Five Minutes to Music History

Fun and Easy-to-Teach Lessons for the Four Musical Eras

This book is dedicated to four wonderful females in my life ranging in ages from 6 to 90
For Olivia, my most beautiful granddaughter
For Jeannette, my son's awesome wife
For Annelle, my fantastic wife and proofreader
For Mary, my marvelous mother

by Rick Weymuth

Shawnee Press

EXCLUSIVELY DISTRIBUTED BY

HAL•LEONARD®
CORPORATION
7777 W. BLUEMOUND RD. P.O. BOX 13819 MILWAUKEE, WI 53213

ISBN   978-1-59235-245-6

Visit Shawnee Press online at www.shawneepress.com

TABLE OF CONTENTS

FOREWORD

Understanding the development of music through history will make your students better listeners and stronger performers! As a music teacher who has taught all levels of music from kindergarten through graduate studies, I have always looked for creative ways to help my students understand and appreciate music history. Since there are few quick and concise music history references for busy junior and senior high school teachers, this reproducible book with the important facts, games, quizzes, and timelines is exactly what you need for your music classroom!

Whether you devote only five minutes or a full hour, you can adapt FIVE MINUTES TO MUSIC HISTORY to your unique teaching situation over a semester or an entire academic year. With a comprehensive layout and reproducible pages, you'll discover how easy this affordable teaching tool is to use in your teaching.

Rick Weymuth

My goal was to take the four major European musical periods— Renaissance, Baroque, Classical and Romantic—and make each time come alive and be of interest to students. In each of the four musical eras, you will find the sections identified with a READY, SET, and a GO!

Let's Learn About the Era   **Let's See What You Have Learned**   **Let's Sing What We Know**

In the READY section, you'll find an introduction to each era, a timeline contrasting what was happening in America at that time, as well as brief biographies about the most famous composers. In the SET section, you'll find worksheets and study quizzes to help students remember key dates, people, and places as well as a unit exam (compiled from questions featured on the study quizzes). The GO! section at the end of each era contains a gem of a reproducible choral for your classes to learn to sing that is indicative of each era of music studied. I chose and edited each to reflect the key elements discussed about each musical period in history.

It was such a pleasure to write this book and my hope is that you and your students enjoy music history together!

Dr. Rick Weymuth
Emeritus Professor of Music
Northwest Missouri State University

THE RENAISSANCE ERA

The Renaissance (1450-1600) was a time of renewal, excitement, and freedom. This period was a contrast to the Medieval Era in which rhythmic music modes rarely deviated and had strict liturgical (church) texts. New and exciting timbres (sounds) that came from combining voices and instruments in new and creative ways were appearing in the Renaissance. During this time, voices and instruments could be used on the same parts, or in any way the conductor chose. For example, if the madrigal had four parts and the conductor had only three singers, an instrument would be used on the fourth part.

Instruments played during the Renaissance were recorders, krummhorns, lutes, viols, and the portative organ. Percussion instruments such as hand drums, tambourines, and finger cymbals were also used. Other than the church organ, the major keyboard instrument was the harpsichord, its earliest reference being 1397. The harpsichord was used as both a solo and an accompanying instrument and was distinguished from the clavichord or piano by the fact that the strings were plucked rather than struck. Similar instruments came in many shapes and sizes – the virginal, spinet, clavecin, and clavicembalo, each with a distinct sound due to shape and string configuration.

> **The male soprano voice was the most important and significant new tone color of the Renaissance.**

While secular (nonreligious) choral music was written to be performed for the courts of the European royal families or guests at special events, sacred choral music was created and performed for the churches, each church or cathedral wanting to have the finest music for their services. Throughout the Renaissance, women were forbidden to sing in the Catholic Church. Only males were permitted to sing. Boys with unchanged voices sang the two highest vocal lines, the soprano and alto, and men sang the lower tenor and bass voices. For example, the Sistine Chapel at St. Peter's Basilica in the Vatican allowed only males to sing in its choir. Boys began their careers as choirboys and typically became choir members, composers, and conductors. Competition for the finest choir became so competitive that it was rumored that the famous child singer (and later a composer) Orlando di Lasso was kidnapped twice by jealous priests because he was such an outstanding boy singer.

> **The use of instruments was prohibited in the Sistine Chapel, thus all music was sung a cappella (without use of instruments or organ).**

The vocal sounds of the Renaissance contained tension that was produced by singers with partially closed mouths. This is obvious from viewing paintings of singers during this musical period. Vibrato in the voices was considered an undesirable trait during the Renaissance. In his writing of the period, Thurston Dart states that little or no vibrato should be used when singing Renaissance choral literature.

Secular (nonreligious) choir music became important in all the Royal Courts of Europe during this time. Choral music of three, four, and more parts was sung by members of the courts. Many times servants were hired to work in the courts because of their singing ability. If the Lord of the manor was a bass, then a male servant was hired to sing tenor and a female servant to sing the part that the lady of the house did not sing.

The evening's entertainment after a bountiful dinner featured the Royal Court and selected servants sitting around the banquet table and singing secular songs. This was the beginning of the Madrigal Feastes, Yuletide Feastes, or Renaissance Dinners. As their popularity grew, all of the Royal Courts wanted this new form of entertainment. Even the lesser lords felt that they needed music after dinner. Composers were hired by the courts to create and perform music during the Feastes. On special Feaste Days, the composers were well paid and were provided housing.

The term "madrigal" refers to a new poetic form in the sixteenth century. Known by its freedom and irregularity, the madrigal typically had four to six voices, and often was an elaborate composition that contained word painting (where the text depicted visual image) and complex vocal lines. Madrigal was the term used in England and Italy for this type of musical composition, but was referred to as a "chanson" in France and a "lied" in Germany.

The invention of the printing press was one of the most important advances of the period. It gave composers a precise way of duplicating their compositions. Prior to that, all music and books had to be hand copied. Music could now be produced much faster and in greater quantities.

Gutenberg

WHAT WAS HAPPENING IN AMERICA DURING THE RENAISSANCE?

The earliest known inhabitants of the United States were Native Americans who played the first music in this land. Music from this time was sung almost entirely in one part or unison. Instruments used during this period were drums and flutes made out of bone, wood, and cane. Because the length of the flutes was not uniform, the pitch of each instrument was different. Therefore, usually only one flute was used at a time to avoid conflicting pitches.

During the Renaissance, Christopher Columbus led his three ships, the Niña, the Pinta, and the Santa Maria, across the ocean. They arrived in America, or what was called the New World, on October 11, 1492.

Famous Composers of the Renaissance

Josquin des Prez

Josquin des Prez (ca. 1450–1521) began his musical career as a choirboy in Milan. He was considered the greatest choral composer of the early sixteenth century and most importantly, his fellow composers felt that he was the "Father of Musicians." During his life, he was a member of the papal chapel from 1486–1495 and later served in the court of King Louis XII of France. In 1505, he composed the Renaissance Italian madrigal, "El Grillo (The Cricket)" (see pg. 16).

Orlando di Lasso (1532–1594), also known as Orlandus di Lassus, was born in the Netherlands, but successfully composed Italian madrigals and frottolas (like a madrigal), French chansons, and German lied. He was also a major composer for the church. Unlike Palestrina, di Lasso traveled widely throughout Western Europe and was considered the most versatile and vigorously creative master of the madrigal and chanson, publishing his first book of madrigals in 1555.

Orlando di Lasso

John Dowland

John Dowland (1562–1626), known as the greatest English composer during the Renaissance, published "The First Booke of Songs and Ayres" on October 31, 1597 because he was upset with Queen Elizabeth I of England. She had twice refused to hire him as the court lutenist (a person who plays the lute, which is a plucked instrument with a fretted neck and a deep round back). Years later, King James I appointed Dowland to that position. He is now recognized as the greatest English composer of music and songs for the lute.

Giovanni Pierluigi da Palestrina (ca. 1525–1594) was named Palestrina after the town of his birth. Considered one of the two major sacred composers of the Renaissance period, he was known for his new and different church music, and for the vast number of pieces he composed. These new styles were passed on to his numerous students and the styles served the church throughout the western world. Giovanni was organist and choirmaster of the principal church of his native city St. Agapito, Palestrina. After the Bishop of Palestrina, Cardinal Giovanni Maria del Monte, was elected Pope Julius III in 1572, he summoned Giovanni to the Vatican to become maestro di cappella at St. Peter's from 1572–1594, which was the highest level a musician could achieve in the Vatican. At the time of Palestrina's death, he was considered the greatest sacred choral composer in Europe. One of the works for which he is most famous is the "Pope Marcellus Mass."

Giovanni Pierluigi da Palestrina

Pierre Certon

Pierre Certon (ca. 1510–1572) was the most important French composer during the Renaissance. As a young man, he attended the very strict school at Notre Dame Cathedral where he got into trouble for playing ball, which was against the school's rules, as well as refusing to attend a church service. The latter was a serious offense and could have sent him to prison, but he was forgiven because of his youth. He was very influential in the late development of the French chanson and in 1536 became a master of choristers at the Sainte-Chapelle, remaining at this post for the rest of his life.

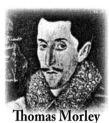

Thomas Morley (1557–1602) was born in England and was a student of the famous composer, William Byrd. An exclusive license for printing music was granted to him by Queen Elizabeth I. For twenty-one years, he selected all the music to be published in England. Active as a composer and publisher, he became the driving force behind the development of the English madrigal. Morley wrote "A Plaine and Easie Introduction to Practicall Musik" in 1597, which was the most important English Treatise on musical performance and composition.

Thomas Morley

Tomás Luis de Victoria

Tomás Luis de Victoria (1548–1611) (sometimes spelled "da Vittoria") was a Spanish composer of the late Renaissance and was the most famous composer of the sixteenth century in Spain. De Victoria, born in Avila, Spain, trained as a choirboy and later traveled to Rome in 1564, where he joined the monastery founded by St. Ignatius Loyola. He was ordained as a priest in 1575. Tomás Luis de Victoria remained in the convent where he served as priest, director of the choir, composer, and organist until the end of his life.

CHRONOLOGY OF THE RENAISSANCE ERA (1450–1600)

1450

1439 Johann Gutenberg invents the printing press.

1450 The Renaissance begins.

1477 Vlad the Impaler (Dracula) dies in exile.

1491 Petrucci is the first to print complete song collections.

1492 Columbus discovers the New World on October 11.

1500

1504 Michelangelo carves the statue "David."

1505 Josquin des Prez writes the Italian madrigal, "El Grillo."

1506 St. Peter's Cathedral construction begins in Rome.

1507 A German map is the first to use the name "America."

1508 Michelangelo begins painting the Sistine Chapel ceiling in the Vatican.

1509 Henry VIII becomes King of England.

1510 First African slaves arrive in the Americas.

1517 Martin Luther nails his 95 theses to the door of Wittenberg Church.

1519 Leonardo da Vinci, painter, theoretician, and inventor, dies.

1540 Hernando de Soto leads the first European explorers into the interior of North America.

1545–63 The Council of Trent provides a basis for reform of the Catholic Church.

1541 Hernando de Soto discovers the Mississippi River.

1548 Tomás Luis de Victoria, considered the most famous Spanish composer, is born.

1550

1555 Orlando di Lasso publishes his first book of madrigals.

1558 Elizabeth I becomes Queen of England.

1560s The lead pencil is invented.

1565 St. Augustine, in what is now Florida, is founded.

1567 Palestrina publishes the "Pope Marcellus Mass."

1577 Sir Francis Drake sails around the world.

1594 William Shakespeare writes "Romeo and Juliet."

1597 Thomas Morley publishes "A Plaine and Easie Introduction to Practicall Musick."

1597 John Dowland publishes "The First Booke of Songs or Ayres."

1599 The Globe Theatre is built in London for Shakespeare's playing company.

1600

1600 The Renaissance Era ends.

STUDY QUIZ #1
RENAISSANCE ERA

Fill in the Blanks

1. The Renaissance began in year _____ and ended in the year _____.

2. Sacred choral music of the Renaissance was created and performed for the _____.

3. Secular choral music was written for the _____ of the European royal families.

4. Other than the church organ, the major keyboard instrument used in the Renaissance was the _____.

5. The period prior to the Renaissance Era was the _____ Era.

6. During the Renaissance, _____ and _____ could be used on the same parts, or in any way the conductor so chose.

7. The most significant new tone color was produced by the voices of the _____.

8. Only _____ were permitted to sing in Catholic churches.

9. In his writing of the Renaissance period, Thurston Dart stated that little or no _____ should be used when singing choral literature.

10. All music in the Sistine Chapel at the Vatican was sung _____ (without the use of instruments).

STUDY QUIZ # 2
RENAISSANCE ERA
Major Composers

Match the correct composer to the information listed.

A. Palestrina

B. Dowland

C. des Prez

D. di Lasso

E. Certon

F. de Victoria

G. Morley

1. _____ was a Spanish composer who was also a priest.

2. _____ wrote the "Pope Marcellus Mass."

3. _____ was the most important French composer during the Renaissance.

4. _____ was born in the Netherlands and was considered the most versatile and vigorously creative master of the madrigal and chanson.

5. _____ was born in England and is known as the greatest lute player of the Renaissance.

6. _____ was born in England and wrote "A Plaine and Easie Introduction to Practicall Musik."

7. _____ was considered the greatest choral composer of the early sixteenth century and his fellow composers felt he was the "Father of Musicians."

STUDY QUIZ #3
RENAISSANCE ERA
Word Find

S	S	R	V	H	Y	D	A	T	K	W	Q	J	U	Z	E	F	D	S	I
T	R	E	B	L	R	P	R	I	N	T	I	N	G	P	R	E	S	S	W
P	Q	B	N	U	X	W	Q	H	K	I	Y	D	Z	S	W	R	T	H	H
E	G	S	E	T	A	O	R	W	D	F	E	U	C	O	P	W	R	D	A
T	Z	A	T	E	Y	U	B	V	A	T	I	C	A	N	E	I	P	T	R
E	W	Z	F	T	U	I	P	D	X	V	E	U	T	C	N	T	D	S	P
R	C	H	R	I	S	T	O	P	H	E	R	C	O	L	U	M	B	U	S
S	S	Q	L	E	F	Z	G	R	S	I	E	S	T	I	N	E	A	B	I
B	I	R	V	L	E	D	E	F	I	R	N	C	F	L	U	T	E	S	C
A	S	V	Z	F	W	R	B	T	J	K	A	E	T	G	V	H	S	J	H
S	T	W	F	H	J	U	V	U	W	T	I	L	A	X	T	P	M	E	O
I	I	T	W	V	T	M	U	Y	V	N	S	E	S	Q	T	T	E	V	R
L	N	E	T	B	X	S	C	T	N	H	S	M	R	R	U	E	D	E	D
I	E	F	R	T	X	T	B	M	R	E	A	Q	C	L	V	G	I	H	A
C	C	M	A	D	R	I	G	A	L	X	N	T	T	Y	F	R	E	Q	K
A	H	C	R	H	Y	I	E	N	V	U	C	K	A	J	S	R	V	M	Z
E	A	Y	U	I	P	F	T	Y	C	T	E	H	A	J	S	R	A	N	A
X	P	Q	D	R	G	U	K	F	V	C	R	J	T	A	Z	H	L	Y	W
G	E	N	N	A	T	I	V	E	A	M	E	R	I	C	A	N	S	T	X
E	L	R	T	B	U	R	E	C	O	R	D	E	R	D	T	B	J	E	B

CHRISTOPHER COLUMBUS

DRUMS

FLUTES

HARPSICHORD

LUTE

MADRIGAL

MEDIEVAL

NATIVE AMERICANS

PRINTING PRESS

RECORDER

RENAISSANCE

SISTINE CHAPEL

ST. PETER'S BASILICA

VATICAN

STUDY QUIZ #4
RENAISSANCE ERA
Word Scramble

CHURCH ORGAN
CLAVECIN
CLAVICEMBALO
CLAVICHORD
FINGER CYMBALS
HAND DRUM
HARPSICHORD
KRUMMHORN
LUTE
PORTATIVE ORGAN
RECORDER
SPINET
TAMBOURINE
VIOL
VIRGINAL

1. CACIEVLN _____

2. COERRERD _____

3. GENFIR LYMABCS _____

4. HARDISPORCH _____

5. HURCHC RANOG _____

6. MICEBOCLAVAL _____

7. NESPIT _____

8. NIRVIAGL_____

9. OILV _____

10. RABOIENTUM _____

11. RATTIPOEV NRAOG _____

12. NHAD RMUD _____

13. RMUNHRMOK _____

14. TEUL _____

15. VAIRDCOCLH_____

STUDY QUIZ #5
RENAISSANCE ERA
Fill in the Blanks

1. The _____ was invented in 1439 and was one of the most important advances of the Renaissance period. It gave composers a precise way of duplicating their compositions.

2. During the Renaissance, Native American music was typically sung in _____ part and had flute and drum accompaniment.

3. The famous child singer and later composer, _____, was kidnapped twice by jealous priests because he was such an outstanding boy singer.

4. _____ (ca. 1450–1521) was considered the greatest composer of the early sixteenth century.

5. _____ (1532–1594) was born in the Netherlands, but successfully composed Italian madrigals, French chansons, and German lied.

6. _____ (1562–1626) was considered the finest lute player of his time.

7. _____ (ca. 1525–1594) was named after the town of his birth. At the time of his death, he was the most revered composer in Europe. His most famous Mass was the "Pope Marcellus Mass."

8. _____ (ca. 1510–1572) was an important French composer during the Renaissance and was very influential in the development of the French chanson. In 1536, he became a master of choristers at the Sainte-Chapelle, remaining at this post for the rest of his life.

9. _____ (1557–1602) was born in England. Queen Elizabeth I granted him the exclusive license for printing music in England.

STUDY QUIZ #6
RENAISSANCE ERA
Word Find

P	B	L	K	M	Y	R	Q	X	N	O	T	R	E	D	A	M	E	N	T
A	F	T	V	B	U	O	Q	A	Z	F	E	B	T	F	J	S	T	J	H
L	E	R	Q	U	E	E	N	E	L	I	Z	A	B	E	T	H	T	D	O
E	A	R	B	Y	U	E	N	O	Z	E	W	N	Y	W	P	Z	R	W	M
S	M	W	D	O	M	I	C	H	E	L	A	N	G	E	L	O	R	I	A
T	X	R	C	Q	R	T	V	Y	G	D	U	J	R	Q	Y	N	X	L	S
R	Q	X	O	P	U	S	H	A	K	E	S	P	E	A	R	E	R	L	M
I	A	V	W	E	C	J	T	X	E	R	A	B	X	W	D	M	E	I	O
N	L	I	T	T	C	O	M	K	I	N	G	L	O	U	I	S	F	A	R
A	W	C	Z	R	P	S	A	G	J	X	E	V	T	N	F	J	S	M	L
X	P	T	C	U	H	Q	T	N	E	V	W	Y	H	E	H	P	R	B	E
W	T	O	Q	C	Z	U	Y	C	E	A	G	P	V	D	V	O	X	Y	Y
M	K	R	E	C	D	I	A	U	C	R	T	A	X	D	S	P	I	R	Q
G	H	I	L	I	R	N	C	Q	Z	E	T	G	D	W	S	E	Y	D	T
J	F	A	K	V	E	O	R	D	W	H	N	A	M	R	X	J	D	R	A
R	T	F	J	O	H	N	D	O	W	L	A	N	D	E	A	U	T	C	Z
S	R	J	E	A	H	T	X	W	M	O	U	X	T	O	U	L	H	C	V
P	I	E	R	R	E	C	E	R	T	O	N	E	T	C	W	I	J	G	A
C	G	U	W	J	R	W	O	U	B	S	E	J	R	K	E	U	V	T	W
N	O	R	L	A	N	D	O	D	I	L	A	S	S	O	Y	S	J	F	H

JOHN DOWLAND
JOSQUIN
KING LOUIS
MICHELANGELO
NOTRE DAME
ORLANDO DI LASSO
PALESTRINA
PETRUCCI

PIERRE CERTON
POPE JULIUS
QUEEN ELIZABETH
SHAKESPEARE
THOMAS MORLEY
VICTORIA
WILLIAM BYRD

UNIT EXAM - Page 1
RENAISSANCE ERA

1. The Renaissance Era began in the year _____ and ended _____.

2. Prior to the Renaissance was the _____ Era.

3. During the Renaissance, _____ and _____ could be used on the same parts, or in any way the conductor so chose.

4. Other than the church organ, the major keyboard instrument used in the Renaissance was the _____.

5. The most significant new tone color was produced by the voices of the _____.

6. In the Renaissance, sacred choral music was created and performed for the _____.

7. Secular choral music was written for the _____of the European royal families.

8. Only _____ were permitted to sing in Catholic churches.

9. The famous child singer (and later composer) _____, was kidnapped twice by jealous priests because he was such an outstanding boy singer.

10. In his writing of the Renaissance Era, Thurston Dart stated that little or no _____ should be used when singing choral literature.

11. All music in the Sistine Chapel at the Vatican was sung _____ (without the use of instruments).

12. The _____ was invented in 1439 and was one of the most important advances in the Renaissance. It gave the composers a precise way of duplicating their compositions.

13. Native American music during the Renaissance was typically sung in _____ and had flute and drum accompaniment.

14. _____ (ca. 1450–1521) was considered the greatest composer of the early sixteenth century.

15. _____ (1532–1594) was born in the Netherlands, but successfully composed Italian madrigals, French chansons, and German lied.

16. _____ (1562–1626) was considered the finest lute player of his time.

17. _____ (ca. 1525–1594) was named after the town of his birth. At the time of his death, he was the most revered composer in Europe. His most famous mass was the "Pope Marcellus Mass."

18. _____ (ca. 1510–1572) was an important French composer during the Renaissance and was very influential in the development of the French chanson. In 1536, he became a master of choristers at the Sainte-Chapelle, remaining at this post for the rest of his life.

19. _____ (1557–1602) was born in England. Queen Elizabeth I granted him the exclusive license for printing music in England.

20. _____ (1548–1611) was born in Avila, Spain where he was trained as a choirboy. He was ordained as a priest in 1575.

Dedicated to Bob Crews and the choir of
Westside Christian High School, Lake Oswego, OR

EL GRILLO
(The Cricket)

for SATB voices, with optional accompaniment

by Josquin des Prez
Arranged by
RICK WEYMUTH

18

PRONUNCIATION

El grillo e buon cantore che tiene longo verso,
Ehl greel-loh eh boo-ohn kahn-toh-reh keh tee-eh-neh lohn-goh vehr-soh,

dale beve grillo canta.
dah-leh beh-veh greel-loh kahn-tah.

Ma non fah come gli altri un celli, come li han cantato un poco.
Mah nohn fah koh-meh lyee ahl-tree oon chehl-lee, koh-meh lee ahn kahn-tah-toh oon poh-koh.

Van de fatto in altro loco, sempre el grillo sta pur saldo.
Vahn deh faht-toh een ahl-troh loh-koh, sehm-preh ehl greel-loh stah poor sahl-doh.

Quando la maggior el caldo allor canta sol per amore.
Kwahn-doh lah mahj-jeeohr ehl kahl-doh ahl-lohr kahn-tah sohl pehr ah-moh-reh.

The Baroque Era began in 1600 and ended with the death of Johann Sebastian Bach in 1750. The three distinct styles of this period were church music, theater music, and chamber music. Known for grandeur, large-scale productions, spectacular ideas and major contrasts, the music, art, and architecture of this time became very important to the wealthy nobility.

During the Baroque period, there were major developments in dramatic music — the oratorio, opera, cantata, and Passion music. The oratorio was a dramatic large-scale production dealing with a Biblical subject. It would have a narrator (soloist), chorus, and orchestra. Unlike opera, no costumes, scenery, or staging was used in an oratorio. The cantata, usually a shorter work limited to soloists, a small number of chorus members, and a small orchestral accompaniment, could be written on either sacred or secular subjects. Passion music specifically centered on the Christian Easter story. Baroque church music departed from the a cappella style of the Renaissance period. Many of the European Baroque church composers wrote their compositions in the local language of the country rather than Latin.

These important new styles created dramatic music. Dramatic music, especially in the form of operas, was first written in Florence, Italy. All forms of dramatic music — including oratorio, cantata, and Passion music — were soon found in Italy, which then spread throughout Europe. In the Roman operas, grand choruses were added. The recitative and aria were added in Venetian operas. The first public opera, "Teatro San Cassiano," was performed in Venice in 1637. In the city of Naples, the Italian overture was added to the opera as a beautiful opening for the production.

In his book, "Historie de la Musique" (1725), Le Cerf de la Vieville states "a perfect voice should be sonorous, extensive, sweet, neat, lively, and flexible." During this time, the vocal bass part came into its own as an important line with the soprano's melodic line. The tenor and alto parts were incidental to these two parts, therefore performed with less volume.

The keyboard of choice was the harpsichord rather than the piano, which later came into its own in the Classical Era. To substitute for the harpsichord, the composer or performer would use the portative organ or a large pipe organ.

The two major composers of the Baroque period were the German composers Johann Sebastian Bach (1685–1750) and George Frideric Handel (1685–1759). Bach was known for his church music and Handel was lauded for his operas and oratorios. In England, the major composer of choral music was Henry Purcell (1659–1695).

While instrumental music came to the forefront (rather than vocal music), there were many important choral composers who made a significant contribution. In Italy, Giovanni Gabrieli (ca.1553–1612) wrote sacred multipart compositions for choir, brass, and organ; Claudio Monteverdi (1567–1643) wrote madrigals and operas; Alessandro Scarlatti (1660-1725) wrote Neapolitan opera; and Antonio Vivaldi (1678–1741) wrote important sacred choral literature.

In France, both Jean Baptiste Lully (1632–1687) and Jean Philippe Rameau (1683–1764) wrote operas, the latter known as the major theorist of the period. Marc Antoine Charpentier (ca. 1645–1704) wrote both secular cantatas and sacred compositions.

The list of German Baroque composers is longer. Heinrich Schütz (1585–1672) was known for his cantatas, oratorios, and Passions; Michael Praetorius (1571–1621) wrote choral music in both the Renaissance and Baroque styles; Dietrich Buxtehude (ca. 1637–1707), like Johann Pachelbel (1653–1706), wrote church cantatas with organ accompaniment.

What Was Happening in America During the Baroque Era

In America, the Baroque Era was a time of colonization. The Jamestown Colony was founded in 1607. Henry Hudson explored the Hudson River in 1609. In 1621, Thomas Ravenscroft wrote the "Whole Booke of Psalms," four-part compositions with texts from the Book of Psalms in the Bible. It is believed that the Puritans were singing the psalms in harmony with accompaniment during this time period. The Puritans were credited with the founding of Boston in 1630.

The "Bay Psalm Book" was first printed in 1640 in Cambridge, Massachusetts. Considering that this occurred only 33 years after the Jamestown Colony in Virginia was founded, it represents an excellent achievement.

Other facts of note are:
- **In 1664, New Amsterdam, known as Manhattan Island, was renamed New York.**
- **Philadelphia was founded in 1682 by William Penn.**
- **The famous Salem witch trials began in 1692.**
- **Yale College was founded in 1701.**

The first singing instruction book in America, "The Grounds and Rules of Musick Explained" or "An Introduction to the Art of Singing by Note," was written by Rev. Thomas Walter of Roxbury and published by Benjamin Franklin's brother, James Franklin, in 1721. Previously, music was learned by rote and memorized. Also in 1721, John Tufts wrote and published the first American music textbook, "Introduction to the Singing of Psalm-Tunes."

In 1723, churches in Boston felt that improving singing was very important. Therefore, the better singers began to sit together in groups. These groups became the first church choirs and were moved to a specific gallery in churches. In 1738, John Wesley founded the Methodist Church in America.

Robert Stevenson's book, "Protestant Church Music in America," was an important resource in American music in which he discussed the importance of the Moravian school of sacred composers in Bethlehem, Pennsylvania. The Moravian school of organ builders was considered the best in the New World and David Tannenberg was considered the best organ builder of the Baroque period in America. The Moravian composers used orchestral accompaniment for vocal and choral music in their worship service and established America's oldest continuing instrumental ensemble, the Bethlehem Trombone Choir. The first American performances of Johann Sebastian Bach's major choral works led to the creation of the Bethlehem Bach Festival.

Famous Composers of the Baroque Era

ITALY

The greatest opera composer was Alessandro Scarlatti (1660–1725) and he was from Naples. His best-known operas were "La Rosaura" (1690), "Teodora" (1693), "Tigrane" (1715), and "Griselda" (1721). He also wrote some 600 church cantatas, 150 oratorios, and numerous other sacred church compositions.

Alessandro Scarlatti

Claudio Monteverdi was born in 1567 in Cremona. His first of nine books of secular madrigals was produced in 1587 and his first opera, "Orfeo," was performed in 1607 in Mantua. The subject matter is the same as the Florentine "Euridice" opera, but his was extended to five acts. In 1613, he became the conductor of Saint Mark's Basilica in Venice. In 1632, he was ordained as a Catholic priest and died in Venice in 1643.

Claudio Monteverdi

Giovanni Gabrieli

Giovanni Gabrieli (ca. 1553–1612) was a famous Italian organist and composer. Born in Venice, he studied with his uncle, Andrea Gabrieli, then traveled to Munich to study with the great Renaissance composer Orlando di Lasso. In 1584, he returned to Venice as temporary organist at St. Mark's Basilica and was declared principal organist in 1585. His composition "Sacrae Symphoniae" (1597) impressed composers throughout Europe.

St. Mark's Basilica was built in the shape of a cross with a balcony in each of the four sections of the cross. Gabrieli perfected the concept of compositions that uses two to four or two, three or four of these sections, which were for choirs, organ, and instrumental ensembles.

> **One of Gabrieli's famous compositions, "In Ecclesiis," was written for 64 parts.**

Antonio Vivaldi (1678-1741), nicknamed "the red-headed priest" because of his vibrant hair color, was the son of one of the leading violinists of St. Mark's Basilica and was educated as both a musician and a priest. In 1703, Vivaldi became ill and was excused from his priestly duties. From 1704 to 1740, Vivaldi was employed at the Conservatory of the Pieta in Venice as a conductor, composer, teacher, and general superintendent. Among his many compositions, which included 49 operas, numerous cantatas, oratorios, and motets, two of the most well known are "The Four Seasons" and "Gloria."

Antonio Vivaldi

FRANCE

Italian-born composer Jean Baptiste Lully (1632-1687) developed a unique overture for French opera. The form of this overture was in three sections. The first section was slow with dotted rhythm, the second section was fast and lively, and the third section was like the first section. This same format was later used by Bach and Handel. In 1653, he was appointed court composer in Paris, France.

Jean Baptiste Lully

Jean-Philippe Rameau

Jean-Philippe Rameau (1683–1764) was considered the finest French musician of the eighteenth century. At age 39, Rameau published the famous "Treatise of Harmony." In later life, he began composing operas. The most famous were "Hippolyte et Aricie" (1733), "Les Indes galantes" (1735), "Castor et Pollux" (1737), and "Les Fêtes d'Hébé ou les Talents lyriques" (1739).

Marc-Antoine Charpentier

Marc-Antoine Charpentier was born near Paris, France, ca. 1643. He traveled to Italy to study painting but met the composer Giacomo Carissimi and began studying music. Eventually, Charpentier was appointed maitre de musîque à la Sainte Chapelle in 1698, which is the highest musical post in France. He held this post until his death in 1704. Two of his major choral compositions were "Missa Assumpta est Maria" and "Messe de Minuit pour Noël."

ENGLAND

Henry Purcell

Born in 1659 in Westminster, Henry Purcell was considered the greatest English composer of opera. His father was a singer in the court of King Charles II and Henry started his musical career as a chorister in the Chapel Royal. He wrote the famous "Dido and Aeneas" around 1689, an opera written for a girl's boarding school in Chelsea. Other important operas were "Dioclesian" (1690), "King Arthur" (1691), "The Fairy Queen" (1692), "The Indian Queen" (1695), and "The Tempest" (1695). In 1669, he became organist at Westminster Abbey, and during his six-year tenure there wrote only sacred music. Purcell held numerous posts in London including the appointment as organist of the Chapel Royal. He wrote such important works as "Orpheus Britannicus," a collection of songs, and "Te Deum and Jubilate." Purcell died in 1695 leaving his wife Frances and three of his remaining six children. He was buried beside the organ in Westminster Abby in London, England.

DENMARK

One of the principal Lutheran composers of the Baroque period was Dietrich Buxtehude (ca. 1637–1707). Born in Oldesloe, Denmark, one of his claims to fame was that a young Johann Sebastian Bach walked 250 miles to hear Buxtehude play the organ. Dietrich helped develop the choral cantata that Bach later perfected. Buxtehude received his major organ position at Marienkirke in Lubeck, Germany, by marrying the former organist's daughter. Therefore, when

Dietrich Buxtehude

he was ready to retire, Buxtehude established the prerequisite that anyone taking his job must marry his daughter! Unfortunately, his daughter was very unattractive and numerous organists turned down this prestigious organ position because they refused to marry her. Following his death, the church continued this rule and the next organist married Buxtehude's daughter!

GERMANY

Heinrich Schütz

Heinrich Schütz (1585–1672) was considered the greatest German Lutheran composer of the middle seventeenth century. He attended university to study law, but was sent to Venice to study with composer Giovanni Gabrieli from 1609 to 1612. Schütz's first opera was "Daphne" (1627), which has unfortunately been lost. He spent the major part of his life as organist and composer at Frauenkirche, a Lutheran church in Dresden, Germany. Fortunately, over 500 of his compositions have been located. Two of his major works were "Psalms of David," and "The Seven Last Words on the Cross." He died at 87 from a stroke and buried in the Frauenkirche.

> **In 1665-1666, Schütz composed his three Passions: "St. Luke Passion," "St. John Passion," and "St. Matthew Passion," demonstrating his talent to convey dramatic events in his writings.**

Michael Praetorius

Michael Praetorius (1571–1621) was the youngest son of a Lutheran pastor in Creuzburg, Germany. His last name was Latinized from the original German name, Schültz. He was a prolific composer who wrote sixteen volumes of "Musae Sionae," a series of over one thousand chorales and songs for the Lutheran church. He served as an organist and Kapellmeister. Praetorius was buried in a vault under the organ in St. Mary's Church in Wolfenbuttel, Germany.

Son of a wine merchant, Johann Pachelbel was born in Nuremberg, Germany, in 1653. Pachelbel's first music teacher was Henrich Schwemmer. His first organ position was at St. Lorenz, occurring at the same time he entered the University of Altdord. Pachelbel was known as an outstanding organist and composer of over one hundred vocal and choral works. He died in 1706 at the age of 52.

Johann Sebastian Bach

Johann Sebastian (J.S.) Bach was born on March 21, 1685, the same year as George Frideric Handel (1685), in Eisenach, Germany. Bach spent his entire life within a forty-mile radius of his birth home. He fathered twenty children from his two consecutive wives and the Bach family lived in central Germany for six generations from 1580 to 1845. This family produced many good, and some exceptional, musicians.

Johann received his earliest musical training from his father, who was a town musician in Eisenach. After his father's death, he studied with his older brother, Johann Christoph, an organist.

> **J.S. Bach composed in all of the musical forms popular during the Baroque period except opera.**

Bach's first three professional positions were as the organist in the towns of Arnstadt, Muhlhausen, and Weimar. Next, he moved to Cothen where he was hired to write music for court entertainment. His last job was in Leipzig where he was responsible for all music at the churches of St. Nicholas and St. Thomas. During this time, he wrote numerous cantatas and other church music. Some of the famous cantatas were "Christ lag in Todes Banden (No. 4)," "Ich will den Kreuzstab (No. 56)," a solo cantata, "Ein feste Burg (No. 80)," and "Jesu der du meine Seele

(No. 78)." Some of his outstanding secular cantatas included "The Wedding Cantata," "The Peasant Cantata," and "The Coffee Cantata." Other important large-scale works include "The Christmas Oratorio," "Magnificat," and the great "Mass in B-minor." J.S. Bach's last compositions were the "St. John Passion" and "St. Matthew Passion," and were first performed in Leipzig in 1724. Bach seemed unhappy with the two compositions, because he wrote many revisions.

With the death of Johann Sebastian Bach, the Baroque period ended in 1750. His compositions were not internationally known at the time of his death and amazingly, many of his works that we enjoy so much today were not performed until approximately one hundred years after his death. Today, J. S. Bach is considered the last of the great German Lutheran composers.

GREATEST COMPOSER OF ORATORIOS

George Frideric Handel

George Frideric Handel was born on February 23, 1685, in Halle, Saxony. Unlike the Bach family, there were no other musicians in the Handel family. As a young man, George pleaded with his father for music lessons so his father grudgingly sent him to Friedrich Wilhelm Zachow. As a result, Handel became an outstanding organist and harpsichordist and also studied violin and oboe. In 1702, he graduated from the University in Halle but, unlike Bach, he never married.

Handel's first music position was as the organist in the cathedral in Halle. He then moved to the cathedral in Hamburg, filling the same position. From 1706 to 1710, he was in Italy where he worked for many of the leading nobility. During this time, he created music in four categories— the secular cantata, Catholic sacred music, oratorios, and opera. At the age of 25, he moved to Hanover, Germany, where he became the Director of the Electoral Court of Hanover. Two years later, his employer, Elector of Hanover, was named King George I of England. For thirty-five years of his life, his principal job was to write operas, which today are not as popular as his oratorios. Interestingly, these famous oratorios were not in the job description given him by King George.

Handel is known as the greatest composer of the oratorio during the entire Baroque period. In 1726, Handel became a naturalized British citizen and moved from his birthplace in Germany to numerous other German cities as well as to Italy and England. People spoke of him as belonging to the English school, German by birth, and Italian by training.

Both Bach and Handel were blind at the end of their lives.

Handel's works that have lasted throughout the centuries are his twenty-six oratorios and are his contribution to Anglican Church music. A few of these were "Acis and Galatea" (1720); "Esther" (1720/1732); "Alexander's Feaste" (1736); "Saul" (1729); "Israel in Egypt" (1738); "Messiah" (1741); "Semele" (1709); "Judas Maccabaeus" (1747); and "Jephtha" (1751). A partial list of Handel operas included "Rinaldo" (1711); "Giulio Césare" (1724); "Tamerlano" (1724); "Rodelinda" (1725); "Orlando" (1733); and "Serse" (1738).

Handel also wrote momentous compositions for national occasions. Some of these included the four "Chandos Anthems" (1720), four anthems for the coronation of George II (1727), the "Funeral Anthem" for the funeral of Queen Caroline (1737), and the "Te Deum" for the military victory at Dettingen. Unlike Bach, Handel's compositions were known internationally when he died on April 14, 1759, in London, England. His last composition was "The Triumph of Time and Truth." Today, Handel's only sacred oratorio, "Messiah," is featured in many Christmas performances. He was buried in Westminster Abbey in London, England.

Chronology of the Baroque Era
(1600-1665)

1600

1600 The Baroque Era begins.

1601 Shakespeare writes Hamlet.

1602 Galileo Galilei discovers the law of gravity.

1604 Shakespeare writes Othello.

1605

1605 Pope Paul V is crowned.

1607 Jamestown Colony is founded.

1606 Shakespeare writes Macbeth.

1609 Henry Hudson explores the Hudson River.

1607 Monteverdi's first opera, "Orfeo," is performed.

1610 Louis XIII is crowned King of France.

1620 The pilgrims arrive near Cape Cod on the Mayflower.

1620

1611 The King James version of the Bible is published.

1621 Pope Gregory XV is crowned.

1630 Boston is founded by the Puritans.

1625 Charles I is crowned King of England.

1636 Harvard College is founded by Roger Williams.

1637 Dietrich Buxtehude is born in Oldesloe, Denmark.

1640 The first music book printed in the colonies is the "Bay Psalm Book."

1643 Louis XIV is crowned King of France.

1643 Marc-Antoine Charpentier is born near Paris, France.

1650

1653 Jean-Baptiste Lully is appointed court composer in Paris.

1653 Oliver Cromwell dissolves the English Parliament.

1659 Henry Purcell is born in Westminster, England.

1664 New Amsterdam is renamed New York.

1660 Alessandro Scarlatti is born in Italy.

1665

1665 Heinrich Schütz writes the "St. John Passion."

Chronology of the Baroque Era (1666–1750)

1666

1682 Philadelphia is founded by William Penn.

1666 Heinrich Schütz writes the "St. Matthew Passion."

1678 Antonio Vivaldi is born in Venice, Italy.

1683 Jean-Philippe Rameau is born in France.

1685 James II is crowned King of England.

1685 J.S. Bach is born in Eisenach, Germany.

1685 G.F. Handel is born in Halle, Saxony.

1689 Henry Purcell writes his opera "Dido and Aeneas."

1690

1689 William III and Mary are crowned King and Queen of England.

1692 The Salem witch trials occur in Massachusetts.

1701 Yale College is founded.

1704 Handel writes the "St. John Passion."

1704 Bach writes his first cantata.

1709 The first pianoforte (later shortened to piano) is built.

1714 George I is crowned King of England.

1715 Louis the XV is crowned King of France.

1724 Bach writes the "St. John Passion."

1727 Handel writes the "Coronation Anthems."

1727 George II is crowned King of England.

1729 Bach writes the "St. Matthew Passion."

1730

1730 Bach writes the cantata, "Ein feste Burg" ("A Mighty Fortress Is Our God").

1738 Bach publishes "Mass in B-minor."

1738 Handel writes "Saul," "Israel in Egypt," and "Serse."

1738 The Methodist Church is founded by John Wesley.

1740

1743 Handel writes "Samson."

1746 Handel writes "Judas Maccabaeus."

1750

1750 The death of Johann Sebastian Bach ends the Baroque Era.

STUDY QUIZ #1
Baroque Era
Word Find

A	S	P	A	C	H	E	L	B	E	L	D	F	G	H
C	Q	W	E	R	T	Y	U	I	O	P	C	L	K	J
Z	V	X	B	C	N	B	U	X	T	E	H	U	D	E
G	H	J	K	L	M	A	C	H	B	E	A	T	S	O
F	V	I	P	U	R	C	E	L	L	A	R	S	D	I
D	I	O	R	C	V	H	B	N	M	A	P	S	S	D
S	V	P	A	R	M	O	N	T	E	V	E	R	D	I
R	A	M	E	A	U	A	S	D	F	G	N	H	J	K
A	L	A	T	C	V	B	N	H	A	S	T	A	A	S
P	D	S	O	A	S	D	G	A	B	R	I	E	L	I
O	I	D	R	C	V	B	N	M	M	E	R	U	A
I	F	G	I	P	O	O	I	D	T	E	R	R	L	A
S	C	H	U	T	Z	A	S	E	D	F	G	H	L	J
U	R	N	S	S	C	A	R	L	A	T	T	I	Y	W
Y	T	M	N	M	B	V	C	X	Z	P	I	U	T	R

BACH	PACHELBEL
BUXTEHUDE	PRAETORIUS
CHARPENTIER	PURCELL
GABRIELI	RAMEAU
HANDEL	SCARLATTI
LULLY	SCHÜTZ
MONTEVERDI	VIVALDI

STUDY QUIZ #2
Baroque Era

True or False

Please place a (T) in front of the TRUE statements and an (F) in front of the FALSE statements.

1. _____ The Baroque Era ended the same year that J.S. Bach died.

2. _____ The opera was a dramatic production dealing with a Biblical subject on a very large scale. Unlike the oratorio, it did not use costumes, scenery, or staging.

3. _____ During the Baroque period, the soprano and bass voices were more important in a choral composition than the tenor and the alto.

4. _____ The keyboard of choice was the harpsichord, rather than the piano, which would come into its own in the Classical Period.

5. _____ During the Baroque Era, instrumental music came to the forefront, rather than vocal music.

6. _____ Gabrieli (1557–1612) was the most famous French composer.

7. _____ The two major composers of the Baroque Era are J. S. Bach and G. F. Handel.

STUDY QUIZ #3
Baroque Era
Word Find

A	T	O	U	L	N	E	N	W	V	S	W	T	F	K
R	A	V	E	N	S	C	R	O	F	T	E	Y	R	L
S	N	P	I	X	M	R	M	E	B	E	R	U	A	Q
D	N	X	O	C	A	M	O	R	A	V	I	A	N	W
F	E	C	P	J	S	T	A	T	N	E	T	I	K	E
G	N	V	A	A	F	U	S	Y	M	N	Y	O	L	R
H	B	B	S	M	G	Y	D	U	A	S	U	P	I	T
W	E	S	L	E	Y	I	F	I	S	O	I	Z	N	Y
J	R	T	D	S	H	O	G	O	D	N	O	X	A	U
K	G	S	F	T	J	P	H	P	F	J	P	C	S	I
L	T	A	G	O	K	X	W	A	L	T	E	R	D	O
Q	Y	L	H	W	L	C	J	Z	G	K	X	V	F	P
W	P	E	N	N	Q	V	K	X	H	L	C	B	G	X
E	U	M	J	V	P	U	R	I	T	A	N	S	H	C
R	I	Y	K	B	W	B	L	C	J	Q	V	M	J	V

FRANKLIN	**SALEM**
JAMESTOWN	**STEVENSON**
MORAVIAN	**TANNENBERG**
PENN	**WALTER**
PURITANS	**WESLEY**
RAVENSCROFT	

STUDY QUIZ #4
Baroque Era
Word Scramble

BACH
BUXTEHUDE
CHARPENTIER
GABRIELI
HANDEL
LULLY
MONTEVERDI
PACHELBEL
PRAETORIUS
PURCELL
RAMEAU
SCARLATTI
SCHÜTZ
VIVALDI

1. LARTACITS _____
2. CHAB _____
3. IGLAEBIR _____
4. RELPCLU _____
5. LDVAIVI _____
6. IRCPHERANTE _____
7. UYLLL _____
8. IROEASPURT _____
9. EBTEUXDUH _____
10. EAMRAU _____
11. ENDLAH _____
12. EINOEMTRVD _____
13. TCZSHÜ _____
14. EHAELPLCB _____

STUDY QUIZ #5
Baroque Era
Chronology

Place an (X) in front of the statement that occurred the earliest in history.

1. _____ The Baroque Era began.
   _____ Louis XIII was crowned King of France.

2. _____ The pilgrims arrived near Cape Cod on the ship, the Mayflower.
   _____ Louis XIV was crowned King of France.

3. _____ Louis XV was crowned King of France.
   _____ The Jamestown Colony was founded.

4. _____ The first Bach cantata was written.
   _____ Henry Purcell wrote his opera, "Dido and Aeneas."

5. _____ Bach wrote the "St. John Passion."
   _____ Monteverdi wrote "Orfeo."

6. _____ Marc-Antoine Charpentier was born near Paris, France.
   _____ J.S. Bach was born in Eisenach, Germany.

7. _____ G.F. Handel was born in Halle, Saxony.
   _____ Henry Purcell was born in Westminster, England.

8. _____ The first pianoforte was built.
   _____ The Methodist Church was founded by John Wesley.

9. _____ Bach published the "Mass in B-minor."
   _____ Handel wrote the "St. John Passion."

STUDY QUIZ #6
Baroque Era

What Was Happening in America During the Baroque Era?

Fill in the Blanks

1. The Jamestown Colony was founded in_____ (year).

2. The _____ was the first book printed in America.

3. Philadelphia was founded in 1682 by _____.

4. The first singing instruction book in America, written by Rev. Thomas Walter of Roxbury, was _____

_____.

5. In 1721, John Tufts wrote and published the first American music textbook, _____

_____.

6. In 1738, _____ founded the Methodist Church in America.

7. The _____ school of organ builders was considered the best in the New World.

8. The Moravians provided the first American performances of _____ major choral works, which ultimately led to the creation of the Bethlehem Bach Festival.

STUDY QUIZ #7
Baroque Era

J.S. Bach
Fill in the Blanks

1. Johann Sebastian Bach was born on March 21, 1685, which is the same year that
   _____ was born.

2. J.S. Bach was the father of _____ children.

3. J.S. Bach received his earliest training from his _____ who was a town
   musician in Eisenach.

4. J.S. Bach composed in all of the musical forms popular during the Baroque Era except
   _____.

5. Bach's first three professional positions were as the organist in the towns of
   _____, _____, and
   _____.

6. Bach did not write church music in the fourth city in which he worked,
   _____, because he was hired to write just music for
   court entertainment.

7. Bach's last job was in the city of _____ where he was responsible for all
   music at the churches of St. Nicholas and St. Thomas.

8. Composers _____ and _____ were blind at the end
   of their lives.

9. With the death of J.S. Bach, the Baroque Era ended in _____.

STUDY QUIZ #8
Baroque Era

George Frideric Handel
Fill in the Blanks

1. George Frideric Handel was born in 1685, in Halle, Saxony, the same year as _____ _____.

2. Handel's first music teacher was _____.

3. In _____, Handel became a naturalized British citizen.

4. G.F. Handel was known as the greatest composer of the _____ during the Baroque period.

5. Handel was employed by the Elector of Hanover, who was named _____ _____.

6. Handel wrote many outstanding and important oratorios. List three of his most important ones:

   _____

   _____

   _____

7. Handel's last composition was _____.

8. Handel was buried in _____Abbey in London, England.

STUDY QUIZ #9
Baroque Era
Match the Composition to the Composer

From the list of compositions below, place the corresponding letter next to the name of its composer.

A. "Dido and Aeneas"

B. "Euridice"

C. "Gloria"

D. "Hippolyte et Aricie"

E. "In Ecclesiis"

F. "La Rosaura"

G. "Mass in B-minor"

H. "Messe de Minuit pour Noël"

I. "Messiah"

J. "Musae Sionae"

K. "The Seven Last Words on the Cross"

1._____ Bach

2._____ Charpentier

3._____ Gabrieli

4._____ Handel

5._____ Monteverdi

6._____ Praetorius

7._____ Purcell

8._____ Rameau

9._____ Scarlatti

10._____ Schütz

11._____ Vivaldi

UNIT EXAM - Page 1
Baroque Era

Fill in the Blanks

1. The Jamestown Colony was founded in_____ (year).

2. The _____ was the first book printed in America.

3. In 1721, John Tufts wrote and published the first American music textbook, _____

   _____.

4. In 1738, _____ founded the Methodist Church in America.

5. "Dido and Aeneas" was composed by _____ in 1689.

6. "Gloria" was composed by _____.

7. "In Ecclesiis" was composed by _____ for St. Mark's in Venice, Italy.

8. "The Seven Last Words on the Cross" was composed by _____.

9. "Judas Maccabaeus" was composed by _____ in 1746.

10. The keyboard of choice during the Baroque was the _____

    rather than the piano, which came into its own in the Classical Era.

UNIT EXAM - Page 2
Baroque Era
Match the Composition to the Composer

From the list of compositions below, place the corresponding letter next to the name of its composer. Each composer may be used for one or more compositions.

COMPOSITIONS

1. _____ "Ein feste Burg (No. 80)"

2. _____ "Chandos Anthems"

3. _____ "The Coffee Cantata"

4. _____ "Dido and Aeneas"

5. _____ "Gloria"

6. _____ "In Ecclesiis"

7. _____ "Israel in Egypt"

8. _____ "La Rosaura"

9. _____ "Mass in B-minor"

10. _____ "Messe de Minuit pour Noël"

11. _____ "Messiah"

12. _____ "Musae Sionae"

13. _____ "Orfeo"

14. _____ "The Seven Last Words on the Cross"

15. _____ "Symphoniae Sacrae"

COMPOSERS

A. Bach
B. Charpentier
C. Gabrieli
D. Handel
E. Monteverdi

F. Praetorius
G. Purcell
H. Scarlatti
I. Schütz
J. Vivaldi

Baroque Era

Match the Composer to His Country of Origin

From the list of composers below, place the corresponding letter next to the name of the composer. There may be more than one composer for a country.

COMPOSERS

1. _____ Alessandro Scarlatti

2. _____ Antonio Vivaldi

3. _____ Claudio Monteverdi

4. _____ Dietrich Buxtehude

5. _____ George Frideric Handel

6. _____ Giovanni Gabrieli

7. _____ Henry Purcell

8. _____ Heinrich Schütz

9. _____ Jean Baptiste Lully

10. _____ Jean Philippe Rameau

11. _____ Johann Pachelbel

12. _____ Johann Sebastian Bach

13. _____ Marc-Antoine Charpentier

14. _____ Michael Praetorius

COUNTRIES OF ORIGIN

A. Denmark

B. England

C. France

D. Germany

E. Italy

UNIT EXAM - Page 4
𝕭𝖆𝖗𝖔𝖖𝖚𝖊 𝕰𝖗𝖆
Bach and Handel
Fill in the Blanks

1. George Frideric Handel was employed by the Elector of Hanover, who became _____ _____.

2. Handel was born in 1685, in Halle, Saxony, the same year as _____.

3. Johann Sebastian Bach was the father of _____ children.

4. George Frideric Handel's first music teacher was _____ _____.

5. Johann Sebastian Bach received his earliest training from his _____, who was a town musician in Eisenach.

5. George Frideric Handel is known as the greatest composer of the _____ during the Baroque Era.

6. Johann Sebastian Bach composed in all of the musical forms popular during the Baroque Era except _____.

7. George Frideric Handel was buried in _____ Abbey in London, England.

8. Bach's last job was in the city, _____, where he was responsible for all music at the churches of St. Nicholas and St. Thomas.

9. With the death of _____, the Baroque Era ended in 1750.

Dedicated to the Cole Camp, Missouri, High School Choirs,
Sandy Schlesselman, Director

BREAK FORTH,
O BEAUTEOUS HEAVENLY LIGHT

for SATB voices, with optional accompaniment

Chorale *by* Johan Schop, 1641
Adapted and harmonized by
J. S. Bach
Arranged by RICK WEYMUTH

Words by
Johann Rist, 1641

45

The Classical Era

Historians differ on the dates of the Classical Era, but here we will define it as between 1750 and 1825. The music of this era is referred to as balanced, symmetrical, and traditional with clarity. Composers of this period would often use the same or similar music at the beginning and at the end of their compositions. A good example is in Haydn's "Missa Sancti Nicolai." The Classical compositions were straightforward without the embellishments that can be found in the Romantic period. During this time, the composers wrote more nonsecular pieces, such as operas that were commissioned by the nobility for their own enjoyment. This is a contrast to the Baroque Era, which emphasized sacred compositions. However, some important sacred compositions written by the key composers of that period are still sung throughout the world.

The Classical Era contrasted with the previous Baroque in many significant ways. The Classical utilized more instruments than either of the two previous periods. During this time in history, musical notations evolved into the modern notations we know and use today in our compositions. Another change was that the compositions were exact as to which instruments were to be played in specific sections. Previously, this had not been done. This was also the first time that instruments were no longer the main focus of the writing. Now there would be compositions with large choral ensembles outnumbering the instrumentalists.

Although it was invented earlier, the piano now became the most important keyboard instrument. Older keyboard instruments, such as the harpsichord and clavichord, were not used as they had been in the Baroque period. Unlike Baroque music that focused on and delivered a single emotion or mood per musical section or a movement, the Classical period used more expression.

The use of a continuous tonality for many measures was a common practice during the Classical Era, as opposed to the continuous change of tonalities during the Baroque. This was accomplished by using three tonal chords — tonic, subdominant, and dominant—rather than a movement or section going from chord to chord.

The most outstanding composers of the Classical Period were Franz Joseph Haydn and Wolfgang Amadeus Mozart. These two men were personal friends who truly admired each other and were influenced by the other's work. Because Haydn lived to the old age of 77 and Mozart lived to only 35, Haydn was born twenty-four years before Mozart, and died eighteen years after Mozart. Both composers were born and lived primarily in Austria and around the Hungarian border near Austria, where many of the great classical music composers were centralized.

What Was Happening in America During the Classical Period?

In a letter to a European friend in 1778, future President Thomas Jefferson wrote that American music was barbarous. This really was not a fair statement because Thomas Jefferson was accustomed to the French Courts and hearing only the best musicians in the world. Most of the American musicians were immigrants from England, German, Italy, and France with little, if any, formal training. Jefferson loved music and dancing and often participated in the performances.

The professional musicians during Jefferson's life had to be versatile. A musician would be expected to teach instrumental and vocal music in addition to teaching dance and fencing. Many plantation owners tried to acquire slaves or indentured servants who were qualified on specific instruments, so an entire musical ensemble could be created.

An important early American composer was Francis Hopkinson, born in Philadelphia in 1737. Hopkinson was considered the first American composer and important harpsichordist. His first secular piece of music was published in the colonies. The song, "My Days Have Been So Wondrous Free," written in 1759, is his most well known. Hopkinson was very involved in politics and was a signer of the Declaration of Independence.

William Billings, born in Boston in 1746, was considered the second American choral composer. A tanner by trade, he was most interested in choral singing and wrote "hymn tune" compositions which were published in "The New England Psalm Singer" (1770) and "The Singing Master's Assistant" (1778). His music is still found in hymnals used today.

In 1762, Benjamin Franklin invented a glass harmonica. This instrument consisted of many different sized glass tubes that produced different tones. It was played by wetting the fingers and moving them around the edges of the glass. As you might imagine, the musician's fingers were often cut during the process. Before playing, Franklin would wait until his wife was asleep. Being awakened by the sound, his wife was said to have called it the music of the angels.

The Moravian brotherhood, which had been so important during the Baroque period, started singing-schools in Bethlehem, Pennsylvania in 1750. Then in 1783, they organized "The Society of the United Brethren for Propagating the Gospel among the Heathen (Indians)." This organization requested, and was given, a land grant from Congress for the Indians in the geographic

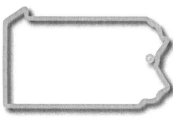

areas we now know as Bethlehem and Nazareth, Pennsylvania. The society lasted until 1823. The Moravians strongly believed that all hymns should be translated into a Native American language. The majority of Christian Native Americans were from the Delaware tribe. The first major Moravian composer of sacred music was George Gottfried Mueller, who came to America in 1784 and taught music at the Moravian Seminary. Mueller sang bass and played the organ, violin, and double bass.

Famous Composers of the Classical Era

FRANZ JOSEPH HAYDN

Franz Joseph Haydn was born in 1732 in Rohrau, Austria, and lived until age 77 (1809). The second child of Matthias Haydn and Maria Koller, his father was a master wheelwright in Rohrau, Austria, near the Hungarian border. Matthias and Maria gave birth to twelve children, the sixth son being Johann Michale, who later became an outstanding singer and composer. Neither of Haydn's parents could read music. Franz Joseph was a self-taught composer and much slower in his musical progress than his friend, Mozart.

During this period, it was a common practice to live with relatives to learn a skill. From the ages of six to eight, Franz Joseph Haydn lived with and received early training on harpsichord and violin from his uncle. At the age of eight, he became a choirboy at the Cathedral of St. Stephen's in Vienna, Austria, and continued to study there for nine years. Some sources say that he was forced out of the choir when he cut the pigtail off the male soprano soloist, his brother, Michael. Other sources say he lost his position after his voice changed.

Franz was taken in by a friend, Johann Michael Spangler, since he had no place to go. During this time, he became a freelance composer and musician, eventually becoming the valet and accompanist for the Italian composer, Nichola Porpora, who recognized his talent.

At age twenty-seven, Haydn was appointed music director for Count von Morzin in Austria. With the security of a full-time position, in 1760 Haydn married Maria Anna Aloysia Apollonia Keller. Like Mozart, he married the sister of the woman that he truly loved. Unfortunately, this was a wrong decision for Haydn as he and his wife shared an unhappy marriage that did not produce any children.

In 1761, the wealthy and powerful Prince Paul Esterházy, a member of a Hungarian noble family, employed Haydn. In 1762, Prince Paul's brother, Prince Nicholas Esterházy ascended to the throne and ruled the Hungarian Province. The Esterházy family had two opulent castles and Haydn lived most of the year in the country palace in Eisenstadt, which had two theatres and two major concert halls. Haydn was responsible for creating all musical performances at both palaces and while at the Eisenstadt palace, he was expected to produce two operas and two concerts each week. His orchestra consisted of twenty-five players and twelve or more singers, some of the finest in Austria and Italy. The professional staff of musicians grew to more than ninety toward the end of Haydn's career.

Between 1796 and 1802, Haydn wrote his best-known choral works. His last six masses were "Paukenmesse"; "Heiligmesse"; "Nelsonmesse" (also known as "The Imperial Mass"); "Hermenegildmesse"' "Schöpfungsmesse"; and "Harmoniemesse" and his last two oratorios were "The Creation" and "The Seasons".

The six masses were all large-scale festival works with an orchestra, chorus, and four solo vocalists. Another very famous mass with orchestra, chorus, and four soloists, written earlier in 1772, was "Missa Sancti Nicolai." Many operas were written while at Eszterháza Palace, but unlike Mozart's operas, they are not well known today. These operas contained many beautiful selections, but not with the outstanding libretti as found in Mozart's operas.

Because of his outstanding contributions to music literature in the Classical era, his fellow musicians gave him a nickname of affection and respect, "Papa Haydn." Another explanation for the nickname was because he lived to the old age of 77. With the average life span in the 40s, his longevity was highly respected, along with his great accomplishments. He was also known as the "Father of the Symphony" and the "Father of the String Quartet." Whatever reason for the titles, Haydn deserved the accolades as a highly accomplished composer of that time.

Many famous graves were robbed throughout history. The prize that the grave robbers typically took was the head of the corpse. Like Mozart and Beethoven, Haydn's head was taken from the cemetery. Fortunately, his head was later found and returned to his grave in 1948.

WOLFGANG AMADEUS MOZART

Wolfgang Amadeus Mozart was born in 1756 and lived to the age of 35 (1791). He was the son of Anna Maria and Leopold Mozart. Leopold worked as violinist, assistant Kapellmeister, and director of the court orchestra of Archbishop Schrattenbach. His mother gave birth to seven children, five of whom died within a few weeks of their birth, which was typical of this period. His only living sister, Maria Anna, was born in 1751 and was fondly nicknamed "Nannerl." Wolfgang was the seventh child and only living son.

Baptized on January 28, 1756, in the Cathedral of Salzburg in Austria, his given name was Johannes Chrysostomus Wolfangus Theophilus Mozart. As a three-year-old, Wolfgang begged to play piano, violin, viola, and organ. He soon became as good as his sister and played new melodies he composed. Mozart was a precocious child genius who was considered a born showman and virtuoso pianist. Cute and bright as a child, he was unfortunately not considered an especially attractive man as he grew older. His nose was larger than normal and it slanted to one side. Smallpox, at the age of eleven, had left his face pockmarked.

Mozart spent approximately a third of his life, 3,720 days, touring as a musician throughout Europe. Never having time to attend school, he was tutored only as time was available. His father would show off Mozart's talent by covering the piano keys with a cloth and requiring Wolfgang to play. In addition, he was required to sing, play duets with his sister, and upon command improvise on various melodies. With his fantastic memory, at the age of 14, Mozart listened to the four and five-part composition, "Miserere" by Gregorio Allegri, which expanded to nine parts in the last movement. Mozart sat down after hearing the composition only once and wrote it down from memory without a mistake. For this task, the Pope honored him with the Order of the Golden Spur. The composer, Johann Adolf Hasse, gave this description of the 14-year-old Wolfgang: "handsome, lively, and charming, with excellent manners" and "one cannot help but be fond of him, once you get to know him."

Mozart was quite stylish. He made up for his looks by his fashionable, elegant, and flamboyant clothing. He loved dancing, and often hosted balls and masquerades at his home. One of these supposedly lasted until 7:00 a.m. He fell in love with Aloysia Weber, but she rebuked him and married an actor. He then married her sister, Maria Constanze Weber, who was born on January 5, 1762 in Zell.

During their nine years of marriage, Constanze gave birth to six children (four boys and two girls) of whom only two lived, Carl Thomas (1784) and Franz Xaver Wolfgang (1791). She was fun-loving and would dance the night away with Wolfgang. Many financial crises occurred in the Mozart family. Wolfgang caused the majority of these problems because he never learned to handle money. He liked to spend money supporting his lavish life-style, which included a gambling habit that he could not control.

The last years before he died were filled with great productivity and major successes like "Don Giovanni," "Cosi fan tutte," "La clemenza di Tito," and "The Magic Flute," all operas that we enjoy today. He became increasingly irritable, his sister-in-law stating "even when he was cleaning his hands, he was pacing back and forth in the room. He never stood still and was always deep in thought."

On November 20, 1791, Mozart experienced swelling in his arms and legs. He had extreme pain and a fever that forced him into bed. Bloodletting was considered a medical cure during the time, by taking ten ounces of blood from him each time. Records show that Mozart had an astounding seven bloodlettings during this final illness. He died on December 5, 1791.

At the time of his death, Mozart was composing the "Requiem (Mass in D-minor, K. 626)," a work commissioned by a mysterious wealthy person, who insisted that his name be kept a secret. After his death, Constanze asked several of Mozart's students to work on the "Requiem" with his student, Franz Süssmayr, eventually finishing the work. Throughout history, people have speculated about that mysterious person who paid Mozart a bag of gold coins (50 ducats) to write the "Requiem," a fact still disputed today. Two major noblemen, Count Vlassic of Stuttgart and Count Franz von Walsegg-Stuppach from the Gloggnitz region, have been suggested as the anonymous men. It was thought that the latter's desire to claim that he wrote the work, not Mozart, was the reason for the mystery. The very popular movie about Mozart's life, "Amadeus," gives one depiction, although there are many aspects questioned for accuracy.

Supposedly, his widow was so poor that it was impossible to give Mozart the luxurious funeral that would have been expected for such a respected composer. It was rumored that Mozart was buried in a pauper's grave, but this is incorrect. Research shows he was buried in a third-class grave, one for the common man. The Emperor stated inner city cemeteries must be closed, and the newest ones were to be of an adequate distance outside the city. When several corpses were brought at the same time, they were laid in the same grave. Typically, the family only attended the chapel service and did not go to the cemetery. Therefore, Mozart was buried in a grave with other bodies in a third-class burial site.

Chronology of the Classical Era
(1750–1825)

1751 First volumes of "Poor Richard's Almanack" are published by Benjamin Franklin.

1756 French and Indian Wars begin.

1769 The steam engine is patented by American James Watt.

1774 The first Continental Congress assembles in Philadelphia.

1776 The Declaration of Independence is signed.

1788 American John Finch invents the steamboat.

1789 George Washington becomes the first president of the United States.

1803 The Louisiana Purchase.

1804 Lewis and Clark departed for their famous expedition of the western United States.

1819 Florida is purchased from Spain.

1750

1770

1790

1810

1825

1754 Samuel Johnson publishes a dictionary.

1756 Wolfgang Amadeus Mozart is born in Salzburg on January 27.

1761 Franz Joseph Haydn is hired by Prince Paul Esterházy.

1763 Excavations begin at Pompeii.

1770 Mozart receives the Order of the Golden Spur from the Pope.

1780 Empress Maria Theresa of Austria dies and her son, Joseph II, becomes ruler.

1791 Mozart dies on December 5.

1798 Haydn writes the "The Creation" and "The Imperial Mass."

1804 Napoleon is crowned Emperor of France.

1815 The metronome is invented.

STUDY QUIZ #1

Classical Era

Mozart and Haydn

Place an (M) in front of statements pertaining to Wolfgang Amadeus Mozart and an (H) in front of statements pertaining to Franz Joseph Haydn.

1. _____ He was born in Rohrau, Austria in 1732.

2. _____ He was born in 1756.

3. _____ His father was the director for Archbishop Schrattenbach.

4. _____ His father was a master wheelwright.

5. _____ His sister was named Maria Anna.

6. _____ He was the only son in his family that lived.

7. _____ He was considered a child genius.

8. _____ He concertized with his sister "Nannerl."

9. _____ He had a brother who also became a famous composer.

10. _____ He married Maria Anna Keller.

11. _____ He married Maria Constanze Weber.

12. _____ He was employed by the wealthy Esterházy family.

13. _____ He wrote "The Creation" and "The Seasons."

14. _____ He died at the age of 77.

15. _____ He was buried outside of the city in a third-class grave.

STUDY QUIZ #2
Classical Era

Instrument Word Scramble

CLAVICHORD   ORGAN

CELLO   PIANO

DOUBLE BASS   VIOLA

HARPSICHORD   VIOLIN

GLASS HARMONICA

1.   AVOIL _____

2.   GNARO _____

3.   ICDORHSPARH _____

4.   LCEOL _____

5.   NOIAP _____

6.   NVIIOL _____

7.   RICHODVALC _____

8.   SASBDOUELB _____

9.   SASGLICAMONRAH _____

STUDY QUIZ #3
Classical Era

Fill in the Blanks

1. The Classical period was defined as _____, _____, and traditional with clarity.

2. The _____ was the most important keyboard instrument used during the Classical Era.

3. The two most outstanding choral composers of the Classical Era were _____ and _____.

4. The dates for the Classical Period are _____ to _____ .

5. Singers and instrumentalists during this time used _____ more as a special effect as opposed to the continuous change in tonalities during the Baroque Era.

STUDY QUIZ #4
Classical Era

What Was Happening in America During the Classical Era?

Fill in the Blanks

1. _____ was born in 1746 and was among the earliest American composers.

2. _____ invented the glass harmonica.

3. _____ loved music and hired slaves and household workers who played specific instruments and sang specific parts.

4. _____ was considered the outstanding American composer and harpsichordist. He also signed the Declaration of Independence.

5. The _____ believed strongly that all hymns should be translated into a Native American language.

6. _____, who came to America in 1784, was the first major Moravian composer of sacred music.

7. _____ was born in Philadelphia in 1737 and wrote the first American secular song, "My Days Have Been So Wondrous Free."

STUDY QUIZ #5

Classical Era

Franz Joseph Haydn

Fill in the Blanks

1. Franz Joseph Haydn was born in 1732 in _____, Austria.

2. Matthias Haydn, his father, was a _____ in Rohrau, Austria, which is near the Hungarian border.

3. At the age of eight, Haydn became a choirboy at the Cathedral of _____ in Vienna, Austria.

4. Franz Joseph sang as a choirboy for nine years. His younger brother, _____, also sang in the Cathedral choir.

5. Franz Joseph and his wife, Maria had _____ children.

6. In 1761, Haydn was employed by the wealthy and powerful _____.

7. In 1762, _____ ascended to the throne. He was a great supporter of Haydn and his music.

8. The Esterházy family lived most of the year in their country palace in _____, Germany.

9. The two most famous oratorios Franz Joseph Haydn composed are _____ and _____.

10. _____was the nickname given to Franz Joseph Haydn.

STUDY QUIZ #6
Classical Era
Wolfgang Amadeus Mozart
Fill in the Blanks

1. Mozart was born in _____ and lived to the age of _____.

2. Leopold Mozart, the father of Wolfgang, worked as violinist, assistant Kapellmeister, and director of the court orchestra of _____.

3. Mozart's only living sibling (sister) was nicknamed _____.

4. Mozart spent approximately a third of his life, _____ total days, touring Europe as a musician.

5. At fourteen, Mozart appeared before the Pope, heard the Gregorio Allegri composition "Miserere" for the first time, and then copied it note for note. Because of this accomplishment, the Pope honored him with the _____ _____.

6. Mozart married Maria Constanze Weber and she gave birth to _____ children during their nine years of marriage.

7. _____ and _____ were two of Mozart's most important operas (there are four possible answers).

8. _____ was the unfinished composition that Mozart was writing when he died.

9. _____ was the student who completed Mozart's final composition.

10. Wolfgang Amadeus Mozart died in_____ (year).

STUDY QUIZ #7
Classical Era

Match the Composition to the Composer

Place an (M) in front of Mozart compositions and an (H) in front of Haydn compositions

1. _____ "Cosi fan tutte"

2. _____ "The Creation"

3. _____ "Don Giovanni"

4. _____ "Harmoniemesse"

5. _____ "Heiligmesse"

6. _____ "La clemenze di Tito"

7. _____ "Nelsonmesse (Lord Nelson Mass)"

8. _____ "The Magic Flute"

9. _____ "Missa Sancti Nicolai"

10. _____ "Paukenmesse"

11. _____ "Requiem"

12. _____ "The Seasons"

Classical Era

Mozart and Haydn

Place an (M) in front of statements pertaining to Mozart and an (H) in front of statements pertaining to Haydn.

1. _____ His father was a master wheelwright.

2. _____ He was employed by the wealthy Esterházy family.

3. _____ He was considered a child genius.

4. _____ He was buried outside of the city in a third-class grave.

5. _____ He had a brother who also became a famous composer.

Composition to the Composer

Place an (M) in front of Mozart compositions and an (H) in front of Haydn compositions.

1. _____ "Cosi fan tutte"

3. _____ "The Creation"

4. _____ "Nelsonmesse (Lord Nelson Mass)"

5. _____ "The Magic Flute"

6. _____ "Missa Sancti Nicolai"

UNIT EXAM - Page 2
Classical Era
Fill in the Blanks

1. The two most outstanding choral composers of the Classical Era were
_____ and _____.

2. The dates used in this unit for the Classical Era are _____ to _____.

3. _____ invented the glass harmonica.

4. _____ was considered the outstanding American composer and harpsichordist. He also signed the Declaration of Independence.

5. _____ was born in Philadelphia in 1737 and wrote the first American secular song, "My Days Have Been So Wondrous Free."

6. At the age of eight, Haydn became a choirboy at the Cathedral of _____ in Vienna, Austria.

7. In 1761, Haydn was employed by the wealthy and powerful _____.

8. The Esterházy family lived most of the year in their country palace in
_____, Germany.

9. The two most famous oratorios Franz Joseph Haydn composed were
_____ and _____.

10. Mozart's only living sibling (sister) was nicknamed _____.

11. At fourteen, Mozart appeared before the Pope, heard the Gregorio Allegri composition, "Miserere" for the first time, and copied it note for note. Because of this accomplishment, the Pope honored him with the _____.

12. Mozart married Maria Constanze Weber and she gave birth to _____ children during their nine years of marriage.

13. _____ was the unfinished composition that Mozart was writing when he died.

Dedicated to the four high schools of the North Kansas City School District
and the outstanding choirs and excellent directors

GLORIA
(from *Missa Solemnis in C minor*, K. 139)

for SATB voices, accompanied, with optional brass*

Music by
Wolfgang Amadeus Mozart
Arranged by
RICK WEYMUTH

Traditional Latin

*Parts for brass can be found on pages 66 and 67

TRUMPETS I & II in B♭

Dedicated to the four high schools of the North Kansas City School District
and the outstanding choirs and excellent directors

GLORIA
(from *Missa Solemnis in C minor*, K. 139)

Music by
Wolfgang Amadeus Mozart
Arranged by
RICK WEYMUTH

BASS TROMBONE

Dedicated to the four high schools of the North Kansas City School District
and the outstanding choirs and excellent directors

GLORIA
(from *Missa Solemnis in C minor*, K. 139)

Music by
Wolfgang Amadeus Mozart
Arranged by
RICK WEYMUTH

The Romantic Era

At the beginning of the nineteenth century, there was clearly a change from the realistic and practical mood of the Classical Era to the Romantic Era (1825–1900) that became more unrestrained and sensuous. The strict rules gave way to a more liberal and fanciful spirit suitable for romance…a change that happened in all aspects of the arts. Music during the Romantic Era was influenced by politics, wars, and new inventions. The French Revolution was over and the Industrial Revolution had begun creating an emerging middle class interested in the arts.

There was now a new sense of nationalism in which composers developed an appreciation of their own country. Previously, the musical influences centered on Italy, Germany, Austria, England, and France. The sphere of musical influence widened. No longer were simple regional folk melodies the only music produced in other countries, but were considered major national compositions written to give the feeling of a united national spirit. These compositions incorporated local legends, melodies, and the folklore of their regions. This was probably greatly influenced by all of the wars going on in the world at that time: Crimean War (1854–1856); U.S. Civil War (1861–1865); Franco-Prussian War (1870). New modes of transportation, such as trains and steamships, moved people throughout the world. Communication expanded because of the recent invention of the telegraph system.

Instrumental colors and harmonic techniques became very important in this Romantic era. New combinations of instruments gave an exciting accompaniment to choral music. Harmonic chromatics or various harmonic tonalities were being used in many of the choral compositions, a major contrast to the Classical Era. These new harmonies gave Romantic music a fanciful and fabulous sound compared to the practical music of the Classical era. Romantic music was an escape from the realities of life.

In 1816, near the beginning of the Romantic Era, a new and important invention influenced all of the composers of this time. The metronome was invented by Johannes Nepomuk Maelzel, setting an objective standard for tempo. Beethoven was the first composer to use this invention.

Franz Schubert and Ludwig van Beethoven began writing compositions that led into the Romantic era. They were considered the crossover composers from the Classical to the Romantic era. Felix Mendelssohn and Johannes Brahms were considered the two greatest choral composers of the new Romantic era. Some other well-known composers included Franz Schubert, Vincenzo Bellini, Georges Bizet, Felix Mendelssohn, Frederic Chopin, Carl Maria Weber, Hugo Wolf, Robert Schumann, and Modest Mussorgsky. All of these composers died at relatively young ages (31–46), which was due to poor health practices and little medical knowledge at that time. The Romantic composers formed a brotherhood, always trying to find ways to hear the works of other composers of the period.

What Was Happening in America During the Romantic Era?

John Tufts' "Introduction to the Singing of Psalm-Tunes" was the first and only American music textbook for many years until Lowell Mason influenced the music scene in America in the 1820s. Lowell Mason was born in Medfield, Massachusetts, on January 8, 1792. He was an extremely gifted musician and began teaching singing at a very young age. In 1812, he moved to Savannah, Georgia, where he was employed by a bank. His extra time was spent teaching singing and he became famous conducting church music and composing. In 1827, he was called to Boston to be in charge of the music for three churches.

Mason became nationally known because of his innovative methods for teaching singing and starting "singing-schools." Typically, singing schools were held during the winter months in many different communities. Mason was determined to raise the standard of singing-school teaching while in Boston. These schools established the foundation for music education as we know today in schools and churches.

In 1834, Lowell Mason created centers that he referred to as an "Academy of Music." His famous "Manual of Instruction in Vocal Music" that he wrote at this time became the official handbook for all singing schools. In 1840, the Academy Convention was organized and officially named the "National Music Convention." Mason was the director of the convention, which was used to train music teachers and singing-school masters. During this time, he wrote hundreds of sacred and secular compositions that were published in over thirty music books. Because of Lowell Mason's influence in so many different areas, the subject of music was the first of the expressive or creative arts subjects added to the curriculum in the public schools in 1838. He was placed in charge of all music education in the Boston Public Schools. From there, his disciples taught the Lowell Mason curriculum throughout the United States. His students introduced the curriculum into the Washington, D.C. schools in 1845 and St. Louis in 1854, the first city west of the Mississippi River to do so. After the Civil War (1861–1865), grade-school teachers throughout the United States added music to their curriculum.

Andrew Law developed a system of musical notations that used differently shaped noteheads for each tone of the scale. This system was known as "Shape Notes" or "Buckwheat Notes." The Shape Note system is still used in some Southern mountain regions of the United States.

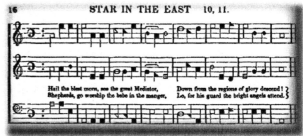

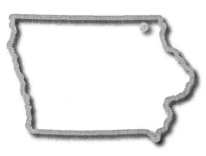

Anton Dvořák, whose most famous composition is the "New World Symphony," came to America in the late 1800s and famously spent a summer in Spillville, Iowa. As director of a conservatory of music in New York City, he was inspired by the music of the New World, especially the songs of Native Americans and African Americans. He combined the rhythms with the folk tunes of his beloved country. Dvořák encouraged his students to use African American melodies for inspiration for their compositions, because he believed that this was the true American music.

Famous Composers of the Romantic Era

AUSTRIA

Anton Brückner

Anton Brückner (1824–1896) was born on September 4, 1824, in Ansfelden, Upper Austria. Brückner's father and grandfather were teachers who taught music at both church and school. Anton was going to follow in their footsteps, but after the death of his father, he was sent to the Volksschule, a primary school, in St. Florian.

In 1840, he moved to Linz to teach and there became a cathedral organist. A music professorship in Vienna, Austria, followed. Anton composed many outstanding choral works, including "Te Deum," "Requiem in D-minor," and "Missa Solemnis in B-flat." Bruckner's "Mass in E-minor" was written for eight vocal parts accompanied by fifteen wind instruments. Bruckner died on October 11, 1896, in Vienna, Austria.

Franz Schubert

Franz Schubert (1797–1828) was born on January 31, 1797, in Liechtenthal, a poor suburb of Vienna. He followed his father's profession as a school teacher, but stopped after three years to follow his dream of becoming a composer. Schubert was the youngest and most prolific composer of the Romantic period. In the year 1815, he wrote two symphonies, two masses, four stage works, 140 songs, one string quartet, two piano sonatas, chorales, and extensive church music. In his lifetime, he wrote 1,240 compositions. Franz Schubert wrote, "I work every morning…when I have finished one piece, I begin another."

Franz Schubert was most famous for his songs. His two most famous used the words from Goethe's poems, "Der Erlkönig" and "Gretchen am Spinnrade." "Die Schöne Müllerin" and "Der Winterrise" are his most famous song cycles, which is a group of songs designated to be performed in sequence as a single entity.

Schubert's outstanding choral compositions include a German Mass, six Latin Masses, five "Salve Reginas" (compositions praising Mary), and two "Stabat Maters" (compositions on the suffering of Mary). Major oratorios are "Miriam's Song of Triumph" and the incomplete "Lazarus." Many of his choral selections featured men's voices.

Schubert died on November 19, 1828, at the age of 31, never having had a home of his own, a permanent music position, or adequate money. He is buried a few steps from Beethoven, in Vienna, Austria.

BOHEMIA

Antonio Dvořák

Antonio Dvořák (1841–1904) was born on September 8, 1841. His father was a butcher, an innkeeper, and also a professional zither player. His parents, recognizing his outstanding musical talents, sent him to music teachers for lessons. At nineteen, he played the viola in the Bohemian Provisional Theater Orchestra. He fell in love with Josefina Cermakova, but following her marriage to another man, he married her sister, Anna, in 1873, and they had nine children.

Anton Dvořák's most famous composition is the "New World Symphony." From 1892 to 1895, Dvořák became director of the National Conservatory of Music in New York City. He spent the summer of 1893 in Spillville, Iowa where some of his cousins lived. During this period, he met Harry Burleigh, one of the earliest African-American composers. Antonio Dvořák died in 1904 and was buried in the Yysehrad Cemetery of Prague.

Bedřich Smetana

Bedřich Smetana (1824–1884), the son of a brewer in Litomyšl, Bohemia, was born on March 2, 1824. He played in an amateur string quartet with other members of his family and studied music in Prague. He was greatly influenced by his friend, Anton Dvořák.

The Czech people had always been known for their beautiful singing and lovely melodies. However, it was Smetana who brought their music to the international level. His comic opera, "The Bartered Bride," utilized the music of the region, the polka. "Dalibor" and "Libule," his serious operas, were not known outside his country.

Smetana left his motherland for Sweden in 1856, and in 1866, he received the job of his dreams, the first director of the National Theater in Prague. Like Beethoven and Schumann, he lost his hearing in 1874 and died of mental problems at the Prague Lunatic Asylum in 1884.

BELGIUM

Cèsar Franck

Cèsar Franck (1822-1890) was basically unknown during his lifetime. He was born on December 10, 1822 in the Belgium town of Liege where he and his brother Joseph entered the Liege Conservatory of Music. At age eleven, he finished his schooling and began touring as a concert pianist. He moved to Paris the following year, becoming a naturalized French citizen. Most of his life was spent in Paris.

Cèsar Franck

In 1855, he became the cathedral organist in Linz where many choral and church works were composed. Two of these compositions were "Ave Maria" and "Les Beatitudes," an oratorio in eight parts. Cèsar Franck died in Paris on November 8, 1890.

FRANCE

Gabriel Fauré

Gabriel Fauré (1845–1924) was born in Pamiers, France, on May 12, 1845, the sixth child of a schoolmaster. At age eight, he was a well-known performer on the harmonium (a portable organ). From 1855 to 1865, he studied at the Ecole Niedermeyer in Paris.

Fauré was most famous for his 97 songs for solo voice, but he also wrote outstanding choral compositions. Some of his compositions included "Cantique de Jean Racine" and the offertory "Tantum ergo."

In hopes of better health, he moved to a small town near Geneva in 1924. Unfortunately, Gabriel Fauré became so ill that he returned to Paris to be with his family and died there on November 4, 1924.

Charles Gounod

Charles Gounod (1818–1893) was born on June 18, 1818, in Paris, France. His mother, a painter, was his first piano teacher and his father was a draftsman. He showed an enormous musical talent and entered the Paris Conservatoire. Later, Gounod moved to Italy to study the music of Palestrina.

From 1870 to 1885, he lived in England. There he became the first conductor of the Royal Choral Society. He wrote many religious compositions and was considered the most gifted among the French contemporaries. His most important opera was "Faust." He died on October 18, 1893.

GERMANY

Ludwig van Beethoven

Ludwig van Beethoven

Ludwig van Beethoven (1770–1827) was born in Bonn, Germany, on December 16, 1770, and his outstanding musical talents were obvious at an early age. When he was eight-years-old, his father featured him in a piano concert, falsely advertising that Ludwig was only six.

He studied with an excellent teacher, Christian Neefe, and in 1783, when his first work was published, his age was listed on the cover as eleven instead of thirteen. At seventeen, when he was on tour with his teacher, his age again advertised as two years younger than he actually was.

The Austrian aristocrat Count Waldstein gave Beethoven a letter of introduction to the elite families of Vienna, who then arranged concerts for him. In 1794, while in Vienna, Beethoven studied with Franz Joseph Haydn for two years. In 1800, Prince Lichnowsky gave him an annual stipend of 600 gulden to stay in Vienna and compose. Beethoven's writings span the end of the Classical period and the beginning of the Romantic period. Breaking away from traditional music and creating his own style, he was considered the first great individualist in music history.

Beethoven was a very unhappy man. According to his letters, hearing loss started around 1796 and continued until 1816 when he became completely deaf. His letters tell us that he distrusted all the people around him, had financial problems, housing problems, and always felt ill. His musical works reflect this dark path into his soul.

Beethoven is considered the most important composer of the nineteenth century. All of his successors were greatly influenced by his compositions. Over 11,000 pages of his written documents, from 1816 to his death, were preserved. One of his greatest works was "Symphony No. 9," in which the last movement was written for choir, soloists, and orchestra. He used a setting of Schiller's "Ode to Joy" in this momentous movement. Two of his other famous choral works were "Christ on the Mount of Olives," and "Missa Solemnis in D." His most famous opera was "Fidelio."

In late 1826, Beethoven felt the end of his life approaching and stated "my work is finished...." The dramatic story is told that during an afternoon blizzard on March 26, 1827, there was a flash of lightning, a mighty roll of thunder, and then he died. Kurt Pahlem wrote "No artist, perhaps, has succeeded more in stirring the imagination of mankind than Beethoven."

Beethoven's funeral was the exact opposite of Mozart's. Thousands of people lined the streets and eight famous musicians were pallbearers. Austria's greatest poet, Franz Grillparzer, wrote the funeral eulogy, and a famous actor delivered it.

Felix Mendelssohn-Bartholdy

Felix Mendelssohn-Bartholdy

Felix Mendelssohn-Bartholdy (1809-1847) was born to a wealthy banking family in Hamburg on February 3, 1809, and then moved to Berlin. Mendelssohn was considered a child prodigy, just like the young Mozart. Felix's sister Fanny Mendelssohn Hensel was also an excellent musician.

The elite met at the Mendelssohn home for weekly concerts on Sunday afternoons. Because his family was wealthy, he had the opportunity to travel around Europe to study. At age sixteen, he composed two outstanding motets, "Exsultate" and "Jubilate."

Considered the most famous composer of the oratorio during the Romantic period, his most well-known oratorio was "Elijah," and the other important oratorio was "St. Paul." At age 20, he found the long lost "St. Matthew Passion" by J.S. Bach and reintroduced it to the world through numerous performances. He died in Leipzig on November 4, 1847.

Johannes Brahms

Johannes Brahms (1833–1897) was born in the northern German city of Hamburg on May 7, 1833 and became a great composer and conductor. He moved to Italy and was captivated by the charm of the country dances and folklore of the region.

He composed many choral arrangements of folk songs. A set of fourteen, published in 1858, was dedicated to the children of Robert and Clara Schumann. He wrote over 200 songs in the traditional German Lied (song) style.

His greatest choral composition was the "German Requiem." Other important compositions included "Ave Marie" (for female voices, orchestra, and organ); "Nanie"; "Song of Destiny"; and "Liebeslieder Waltzes" (No. 52 and No. 65 for solo quartet and four-hand piano). One of his most recognized pieces is "Wiegenlied (Op. 49, No. 4)," also known as "Brahms' Lullaby." Brahms and Mendelssohn were considered the two greatest choral composers of the late 1800s. Brahms died April 3, 1897.

Robert Schumann

Robert Schumann (1810–1856) was born on June 8, 1810, in Zwickau, Saxony. The fifth and last child of the family, Schumann obtained his secondary education at the Athenee de Luxembourg Secondary School. He studied in four different German universities and received his law degree.

Schumann became a virtuoso pianist in Europe and when a hand injury prevented him from continuing playing, he spent more time on his compositions. In 1834, he started "Die Neue Zeitschrift für Musick" (New Journal in Music). His famous secular oratorio was "Das Paradies und die Peri" (1844) and his greatest choral composition was "Mass in C-minor." In 1840, Robert married fellow composer, Clara Wieck. He referred to this time as the "year of song," during which he wrote 127 songs, many his finest works.

Clara Schumann

Richard Wagner

Though born in Leipzig, Austria on May 22, 1813, Richard Wagner (1813–1883) was known as a German composer. Considered the most battle-scarred and controversial composer of the Romantic period, his peers called him a vain and unprincipled egotist. Some of his most outstanding operas were "Tannhauser," "Lohengrin," "Parsifal," and "The Flying Dutchman." Many historians felt that Wagner towered over all other Romantic opera composers. He wrote the huge opera "Der Ring des Nibelungen," which is comprised of four operas: "Das Rheingold," "Die Walküre," "Siegfried," and "Götterdämmerung."

Richard Wagner

In 1849, Wagner went into exile for 12 years because of his alleged membership in anarchist circles. Franz Liszt found him in Weimar, helped him during this time period, and they later went to Zurich, Switzerland together.

In 1864, the young King Ludwig II of Bavaria became Wagner's patron. He paid all of Wagner's debts, gave him amnesty for his alleged involvement in anarchist circles, and moved him to Munich. In 1876, King Ludwig made Wagner's dreams come true by creating The Bayreuth Festival Playhouse in Bayreuth, Germany, where Wagner insisted that King Ludwig provide the best available performers and the largest orchestras. Richard Wagner died of a heart attack in the Palazzo Vendramin on the Grand Canal in Venice on February 13, 1883. His body was returned to Bayreuth and buried in the garden of the Villa Wahnfried.

ITALY

Vincenzo Bellini

Vincenzo Bellini

Vincenzo Bellini (1801–1835) was born in Catania, Sicily, on November 3, 1801. Born into a musical family, he was considered a child prodigy, beginning his piano lessons at age three. By five he was so accomplished, he was playing concerts.

Bellini spent 1827 to 1833 in Milan at the La Scala Opera. He wrote almost exclusively for the opera stage and his opera melodies were spoken of as being warm and flowing, but all in a serious style.

Vincenzo wrote only ten operas in his short career. His major operas included "La Sonnambula" (1813), "Norma" (1832), and "I Puritani" (1834). He died in Puteaux, near Paris, of acute inflammation of the intestine. After burial, his remains were moved to the Cathedral of Catania in Italy, in 1876.

Georges Bizet

Alexandre César Léopold Bizet (1838–1875) was born in Paris, France, on October 25, 1838, but was known by his baptized name, Georges Bizet. Prior to his tenth birthday, he was accepted at the Paris Conservatory of Music.

His most famous composition, the colorful opera "Carmen," was written in 1875. Fellow composer Johannes Brahms attended over twenty performances of the opera and stated that it was the greatest opera produced in Europe since the Franco-Prussian War.

Georges Bizet

Bizet died of a heart attack at the age of 36, a few months after "Carmen" was premiered, so he unfortunately did not know of the tremendous accolades for his opera. He was buried in Paris, France, in 1875.

Domenico Gaetano Maria Donizetti

Domenico Gaetano Maria Donizetti

Gaetano Donizetti (1797–1848) was born on November 29, 1797, the third son of a very poor family that had no training in music. Donizetti was not especially successful as a choirboy but was allowed to enroll in the Lezioni Caritatevoli School on full scholarship.

The third and least important Italian opera composer of the first half of the Romantic Era, Donizetti was considered less gifted than Bellini, but yet he still wrote over seventy operas. The best-known Donizetti operas are "Lucia di Lammermoor" (1835), "The Daughter of the Regiment" (1840), and "Don Pasquale" (1843). His fame in Italy and throughout Europe was instantaneous.

Donizetti married Virginia Vasselli and had three children, none of whom survived. His physical and mental illnesses required him to be institutionalized in Paris, and his death followed in 1848 in his hometown of Bergamo.

Gioachino Antonio Rossini

Gioachino Rossini (1792–1868) was born in Pesaro on February 29, 1792. All of the members of his family were local musicians. His father played horn and was inspector of slaughterhouses and his mother was a singer and worked as a baker. At the age of six, he played triangle in his father's band. Rossini's first wife died in 1845 and he later married Olympe Pelissier.

Rossini was the principal Italian composer during the early Romantic period. He had a good wit and was more successful in the comic opera style than in serious opera. Between the ages of eighteen and thirty, Rossini wrote thirty-nine operas, two oratorios, twelve cantatas, two symphonies, and other compositions.

Gioachino Antonio Rossini

His main works were "L'Italiana in Algieri" (1813), "The Barber of Seville" (1816), and "William Tell" (1829). His most well-known composition was "Stabat Mater," a work in the operatic dramatic style.

After his death at his country home at Passy, Italy, on November 13, 1868, his body was eventually moved to Paris. In 1887, his remains were moved to the Basilica di Santa Croce di Firenze in Florence, where they now rest.

Giuseppe Verdi

Giuseppe Verdi

Giuseppe Verdi (1813–1901) was not known outside his homeland. Considered the greatest Italian composer of the Romantic period, Verdi was born the same year as Wagner, 1813, on October 10, in Roncole, which is close to Parma, Italy.

At age 19, he went to the Milan Conservatory to study, but was not accepted. He wrote 29 operas, one of which he burned—"King Lear." His first four operas were performed in Milan between 1839 and 1843.

The first performance of "Rigoletto" was in Venice on March 11, 1851, followed by "Il Trovatore" (1853), "La Traviata" (1853) in Rome, "Aida" (1871–1872) and "Otello"(1877). Later he composed the opera "Falstaff" and the "Manzoni Requiem." Manzoni was a famous Italian writer whose poems, plays, and novels spoke directly to the Italian people. After Manzoni's death on May 22, 1873, Verdi decided to compose the "Manzoni Requiem" in his honor. This was a huge composition, which is deeply moving and vividly dramatic. It was premiered on the first anniversary of Manzoni's death and is known as Verdi's most famous choral composition. His last public appearance was at St. Mark's in Venice, in 1844, when he conducted this Requiem.

RUSSIA

The Russian Five

Russia came to the forefront musically in the Romantic Era. The country was comprised of many languages and many ethnic groups. Prior to the Romantic period, Russians primarily played their folk melodies and music in the Russian Orthodox Church. The people of this vast country enjoyed singing and especially revered the Russian bass voice with its rich deep tones.

There were five famous Russian composers who were good friends. Referred to as the "Russian Five" or the "Mighty Handful," they were Mili Balakirev, Alexander Borodin, César Cui, Modest Mussorgsky, and Nicolai Rimsky-Korsakov. None had planned a music career, but all were so talented that they followed their hearts into a music vocation or avocation.

Mili Balakirev

Mili Balakirev (1837–1910), whose family was extremely poor, was born on January 2, 1837, at Nizhny Novgorod. Alexander Oulibichev, a Russian nobleman, discovered Balakirev's talent and sent him to the university.

He went to St. Petersburg in 1855 to study with Glinka, a Russian nationalist and opera composer. Balakirev's major choral composition was "Cantata on the Inauguration of the Glinka Memorial," written for chorus and orchestra in honor of his mentor. Balakirev died on May 29, 1910.

Mili Balakirev

Alexander Porfiryevich Borodin

Alexander Porfiryevich Borodin

Alexander Borodin (1833–1887), whose major opera was "Prince Igor," was born November 12, 1833, in St. Petersburg, Russia. His good education included piano lessons. Eventually, Alexander earned a doctorate in medicine at the Medico-Surgical Academy and became a physician and chemist.

He enjoyed dancing and on February 27, 1887, during a ball, he collapsed suddenly and died of heart failure. He was buried in St. Petersburg.

> In 1862, Balakirev met Borodin who is credited for organizing "The Russian Five,"
> a group that promoted Russian nationalism in music.

César Antonovich Cui

Cèsar Cui

César Antonovich Cui (1835–1918) was born on January 6, 1835, in Vilnius, Lithuania. The youngest of five children, César grew up learning French, Russian, Polish, and Lithuanian. At sixteen, he went to St. Petersburg to attend Chief Engineering School, where he achieved the rank of General.

César Cui composed music as an avocation, and studied piano as a young man. While he was a student at St. Petersburg, he found time to take lessons in music theory. In 1856, he met Mili Balakirev and became more serious about composing. His famous operas were "Prisoner of the Cansasus," "William Ralcliff," and "Henry VIII."

Cui was also a music critic who wrote over 800 articles between 1864 and 1918. In 1916, Cui became blind and later died on March 13, 1918. He was buried with the "The Russian Five" in St. Petersburg.

Modest Mussorgsky

Modest Mussorgsky

Modest Mussorgsky (1839–1881), born March 21, 1839, started a military career, but later resigned his military position in order to accomplish other endeavors. He had never studied music but was tormented by musical ideas at night. While in this tormented period of his life, he composed the famous opera "Boris Godunov" and wrote "Songs and Dances of Death." He was found drunk in the street in 1881 and was taken to a hospital that did not diagnosis or treat him correctly. He died at the age of 46 on the anniversary of his birth.

Nicolai Andreyevich Rimsky-Korsakov

Nicolai Andreyevich Rimsky-Korsakov

Nicolai Rimsky-Korsakov (1844–1908) was born in Kikhvin, Russia, on March 6, 1844. His aristocratic family thought that music was not a good profession for their son so they enrolled him in the School for Mathematical and Navigational Sciences in St. Petersburg.

At sixteen, Rimsky-Korsakov admitted that he truly wanted to be involved in music, yet he became an officer in the navy. When not on duty, he composed music.

In July of 1872, Rimsky-Korsakov married Nadezhda Purgold, with Mussorgsky as his best man. Nicolai and Nadezhda had seven children. While still in the navy, Rimsky-Korsakov was appointed a professor. In 1873, he was appointed to a new post made especially for him, Inspector of Music Bands of the Navy Department.

Rimsky-Korsakov was the youngest of the "The Five," but considered the most mature and disciplined. His operas include "The Tale of Sadko," "Tsar Saltan," and "The Snow Maiden." He was known for his exciting orchestrations.

Later, Rimsky-Korsakov's severe cases of angina prevented him from working. He died in Lyubensk in 1908.

Chronology of the Romantic Era
(1825-1865)

1825 The Romantic Era begins.

1827 Ludwig van Beethoven dies on March 27.

1828 Franz Schubert dies on November 19 at the age of 31.

1829 Gioachino Rossini writes the opera "William Tell."

1830

1833 Johannes Brahms is born in Hamburg.

1837 Queen Victoria is crowned in England.

1845 Gabriel Fauré is born in Pamiers, France.

1846 Felix Mendelssohn writes "Elijah."

1847 Felix Mendelssohn dies in Leipzig.

1849 Anton Brückner writes "Requiem in D-minor."

1850

1853 Giuseppe Verdi writes the operas "Il Trovatore" and "La Traviata."

1858 Covent Garden (Royal Opera House) opens in London, England.

1864 Lewis Carroll writes "Alice in Wonderland."

1825

1825 The Erie Canal opens.

1826 James Fenimore Cooper writes "Last of the Mohicans."

1827 The Mormon Church is founded by Joseph Smith.

1827 Lowell Mason moves to Boston to teach in singing-schools.

1838 Music is added to the curriculum of the Boston Public Schools.

1839 The New York Philharmonic Society is founded.

1840 First incandescent electric bulb.

1844 First telegraph message is transmitted.

1850

1851 Herman Melville writes the book "Moby Dick."

1861 The Civil War begins in the United States.

1863 Abraham Lincoln delivers the Gettysburg Address.

1865 The Civil War ends in the United States.

1865

Chronology of the Romantic Era
(1866-1900)

1866

1867 Alaska is purchased from Russia.

1868 Johannes Brahms writes "German Requiem."

1868 Gioachino Rossini dies.

1869 The first transcontinental railroad is opened.

1870

1871 Giuseppe Verdi writes the opera "Aida."

1875 Bizet writes the opera "Carmen."

1876 The telephone is invented by Alexander Graham Bell.

1877 Thomas Edison invents the phonograph.

1881 Czar Alexander II is assassinated.

1883 The Metropolitan Opera opens in New York.

1883 Richard Wagner dies on February 13.

1884 The Bohemian composer, Bedřich Smetana, dies.

1886 The Statue of Liberty is unveiled in New York Harbor.

1889 The Eiffel Tower is completed in Paris, France.

1891 Sir Arthur Conan Doyle writes The Adventures of Sherlock Holmes.

1890

1890 The Belgian composer, César Franck, dies in Paris, France.

1896 Anton Brückner dies in Vienna, Austria.

1897 John Philip Sousa writes "The Stars and Stripes Forever."

1900

1900 The Romantic Era ends.

STUDY QUIZ #1
Romantic Era
Word Find

Q	W	B	O	R	O	D	I	N	E	R	T	Y	G	U
I	O	A	P	A	S	D	F	G	H	J	K	R	L	L
Z	X	L	C	R	U	S	S	I	A	V	B	I	I	N
M	Q	A	W	E	R	T	Y	U	I	O	P	M	N	A
S	D	K	F	G	M	U	S	S	O	R	G	S	K	Y
C	U	I	K	L	Z	X	C	V	B	N	M	K	A	Q
W	E	R	R	T	Y	U	I	O	P	B	A	Y	S	D
F	B	E	E	T	H	O	V	E	N	O	G	K	H	J
K	L	V	Z	U	X	C	V	B	N	S	M	O	Q	W
E	R	T	Y	F	U	I	O	P	A	T	S	R	D	F
G	H	J	K	T	L	Z	X	C	V	O	B	S	N	M
Q	W	E	R	S	Y	U	I	O	P	N	A	A	S	D
F	L	A	W	G	H	J	K	L	Z	X	C	K	V	B
N	M	Q	W	E	R	T	Y	U	M	A	S	O	N	I
O	S	P	I	L	L	V	I	L	L	E	A	V	S	D

BALAKIREV	CUI	RIMSKY-KORSAKOV
BEETHOVEN	GLINKA	RUSSIA
BORODIN	LAW	SPILLVILLE
BOSTON	MASON	TUFTS
	MUSSORGSKY	

STUDY QUIZ #2
Romantic Era
True or False

Place a (T) in front of the TRUE statements and an (F) in front of the FALSE statements.

1. _____ Music was influenced by politics, wars, and new inventions during the Romantic Era.

2. _____ The metronome was invented by Johannes Maelzel in 1896.

3. _____ Beethoven was the first composer to use the metronome.

4. _____ Brahms and Mendelssohn were considered the crossover composers between the Classical and Romantic periods.

5. _____ An emerging middle class was interested in the arts during the Romantic Era.

6. _____ During the Romantic Era, a new sense of nationalism was developing.

7. _____ Instrumental colors and harmonic techniques became very important during the Romantic Era.

8. _____ Schubert and Beethoven were considered the two greatest choral composers of the Romantic Era.

9. _____ Schubert, Bellini, and Bizet all died at relatively young ages.

STUDY QUIZ #3
Romantic Era
Word Find

B	R	U	C	K	N	E	R	S	Q	W	E	R	V	T
R	Y	U	I	O	P	A	S	C	D	F	G	H	E	J
A	K	F	R	A	N	C	K	H	Z	X	C	V	R	B
H	N	M	Q	W	E	R	T	U	Y	U	I	O	D	P
M	A	S	D	F	G	H	J	M	K	B	L	Z	I	X
S	C	H	U	B	E	R	T	A	C	I	V	B	N	M
Q	W	E	R	T	Y	D	O	N	I	Z	E	T	T	I
A	D	S	D	F	G	W	H	N	J	E	K	L	Z	X
X	V	C	V	B	N	A	M	W	Q	T	E	R	T	Y
G	O	U	N	O	D	G	U	I	O	P	A	S	D	F
G	R	H	J	K	L	N	Z	X	C	V	B	N	M	Q
F	A	U	R	E	W	E	E	R	T	Y	U	I	O	P
A	K	S	D	F	G	R	O	S	S	I	N	I	H	J
M	E	N	D	E	L	S	S	O	H	N	K	L	Z	X
B	E	L	L	I	N	I	X	S	M	E	T	A	N	A

BELLINI	DVOŘÁK	SCHUBERT
BIZET	FAURÉ	SCHUMANN
BRAHMS	FRANCK	SMETANA
BRUCKNER	GOUNOD	VERDI
DONIZETTI	MENDELSSOHN	WAGNER
	ROSSINI	

STUDY QUIZ #4
Romantic Era

Music in America Word Scramble

BUCKWHEAT NOTES
DVOŘÁK
LAW
MEDFIELD
MASON
SHAPE NOTES

SINGING SCHOOLS
ST. LOUIS
SPILLVILLE
TUFTS
SAVANNAH

1. _____ LINGHOINSCSGSO

2. _____ FUTTS

3. _____ WAL

4. _____ HNECTWESKBOAUT

5. _____ ARDVOK

6. _____ NAHANAVS

7. _____ ITOSULS

8. _____ SOMAN

9. _____ PEESANHOTS

10. _____ DEEMFILD

11. _____ PLILVLILES

STUDY QUIZ #5
Romantic Era
Chronology
Place an (X) in front of the statement that occurred earliest in history.

1. _____ The Romantic Era begins.
   _____ Johannes Brahms was born in Hamburg.

2. _____ Czar Alexander II was assassinated.
   _____ Queen Victoria was crowned in England.

3. _____ John Philip Sousa wrote "The Stars and Stripes Forever."
   _____ Felix Mendelssohn-Bartholdy wrote "Elijah."

4. _____ Richard Wagner died on February 13.
   _____ Franz Schubert died on November 19.

5. _____ Thomas Edison invents the phonograph.
   _____ First transcontinental railroad opened.

6. _____ Bizet wrote the opera "Carmen."
   _____ Verdi wrote the opera "Aida."

7. _____ Herman Melville wrote the book "Moby Dick."
   _____ James Fenimore Cooper wrote the book "Last of the Mohicans."

8. _____ Giuseppe Verdi wrote the opera "La Traviata."
   _____ Johannes Brahms wrote "A German Requiem."

9. _____ The Eiffel Tower construction was completed in Paris, France.
   _____ The Civil War ends in the United States.

10. _____ Music was added to the curriculum of Boston Public Schools.
    _____ Abraham Lincoln delivered the Gettysburg Address.

STUDY QUIZ #6
Romantic Era

Fill in the Blanks

1. John Tufts' _____
was the first and only American music textbook until the time of Lowell Mason.

2. Lowell Mason was known because of his innovative methods for teaching singing that were
referred to as _____.

3. The singing-schools established the foundation for music education in the
_____ and _____ that we know today.

4. In 1834, Lowell Mason created centers that he referred to as an _____
_____.

5. The subject of music was the first of the expressive or creative arts subjects to be added to the
curriculum in the Boston public schools in the year _____.

6. _____ was the first city west of the Mississippi River to add music to
its public school curriculum.

7. _____ developed a system of musical notation that used shape
notes for each tone of the scale.

8. Anton Dvořák came to America in the late 1800s. During this time, he composed for the
school and community of _____, Iowa.

STUDY QUIZ #7
Romantic Era
Ludwig van Beethoven
Fill in the Blanks

1. Ludwig van Beethoven was born in _____ (city), Germany.

2. When Beethoven was eight, his father featured him in a piano concert, falsely advertising that he was only _____ (age).

3. In _____, (year) Beethoven's first work was published.

4. The Austrian aristocrat, _____, gave Beethoven a letter of introduction to the elite families of Vienna.

5. In _____, Prince Lichnowsky gave him an annual stipend of 600 gulden to stay in Vienna and compose.

6. One of Beethoven's greatest works was _____, in which the last movement was written for choir, soloists, and orchestra.

7. Beethoven's most famous opera was _____.

8. "Missa Solemnis in D" and "_____
   _____" were Beethoven's two famous choral compositions.

9. Beethoven died in _____ (year).

STUDY QUIZ #8
Romantic Era

Composers
Fill in the Blanks

1. The famous Romantic period oratorios, "St. Paul" and "Elijah," were composed by
   _____-_____.

2. _____ was born the same year as Wagner and composed the
   "Manzoni Requiem."

3. _____ composed the choral work "Cantique de Jean Racine" and
   died in Paris, France on November 4, 1924.

4. _____ was born in Hamburg in 1833.

5. From 1824 to 1895, _____ became director of the National
   Conservatory of Music in New York City.

6. _____ moved from France to Italy to study the music of Palestrina
   and later wrote the opera, "Faust."

7. _____ was the great opera composer who wrote "Der Ring des
   Nibelungen" and had King Ludwig II of Bavaria as his patron.

8. In the year 1815, _____ wrote two symphonies, two
   masses, four stage works, 140 songs, one string quartet, two piano sonatas, chorales, and
   extensive church music.

9. _____ was born in Hamburg, Germany, and wrote
   "German Requiem."

10. _____ wrote the "Liebeslieder Waltzes."

STUDY QUIZ #9
Romantic Era

Match the Composition to the Composer

From the list of compositions below place the corresponding letter next to the name of its composer. Each letter may be used one or more times.

A. Mili Balakirev
B. Ludwig van Beethoven
C. Alexander Borodin
D. Johannes Brahms
E. Gabriel Fauré
F. Felix Mendelssohn-Bartholdy

G. Gioachino Rossini
H. Franz Schubert
I. Bedřich Smetana
J. Richard Wagner
K. Giuseppe Verdi

1. _____ "Miriam's Song of Triumph"
2. _____ "The Barber of Seville" and "Stabat Mater"
3. _____ "Christ on the Mount of Olives"
4. _____ "Elijah"
5. _____ "Aida"
6. _____ "The Flying Dutchman"
7. _____ "The Bartered Bride"
8. _____ "Symphony No. 9" with a choral last movement
9. _____ "German Requiem"
10. _____ "Prince Igor"
11. _____ "Cantique de Jean Racine"
12. _____ "St. Paul"
13. _____ "Liebeslieder Waltzes"
14. _____ "Manzoni Requiem"
15. _____ "Nanie"
16. _____ "Fidelio" and "Missa Solemnis in D"
17. _____ "Cantata on the Inauguration of the Glinka Memorial"

STUDY QUIZ #10
Romantic Era
Famous Composers
Word Scramble

BELLINI	GOUNOD
BIZET	MENDELSSOHN
BRAHMS	ROSSINI
BRUCKNER	SCHUBERT
DONIZETTI	SCHUMANN
DVOŘÁK	SMETANA
FAURÉ	VERDI
FRANCK	WAGNER

1. _____ REDIV

2. _____ NOTEDITIZ

3. _____ RAUFÉ

4. _____ NEEDSOHMLNS

5. _____ ÁDVOŘK

6. _____ HUMANCNS

7. _____ NFKACR

8. _____ TAMESAN

9. _____ TIBEZ

10. _____ BUHECTRS

11. _____ HRAMBS

12. _____ GENWAR

13. _____ LELIBIN

14. _____ KRUNCERB

15. _____ DOGNUO

16. _____ SOIRNIS

UNIT EXAM - Page 1
Romantic Era
Beethoven, Brahms, and Mendelssohn
Fill in the blanks

1. Beethoven was the first composer to use the _____, which was invented by Johannes Maelzel in 1816.

2. When Beethoven was eight, his father featured him in a piano concert, yet his family falsely advertised that he was only _____ (age).

3. One of Ludwig van Beethoven's greatest works was "_____," in which the last movement was written for choir, soloists, and orchestra.

4. The Austrian aristocrat _____ gave Beethoven a letter of introduction to the elite families of Vienna.

5. Ludwig van Beethoven's most famous opera was "_____."

6. _____ and _____ were considered the two greatest choral composers of the Romantic era.

7. _____ wrote the following two oratorios "Elijah" and "St. Paul."

8. _____ was born in Hamburg, Germany, and wrote "German Requiem."

9. _____ wrote the "Liebeslieder Waltzes."

10. _____ was from a wealthy family that gave concerts each Sunday in their home, giving him a venue for performance and a way to introduce his compositions.

UNIT EXAM - Page 2
Romantic Era

Match That Composition to the Composer

From the list of compositions below place the corresponding letter next to the name of its composer. Each composer may be used for one or more compositions.

COMPOSERS

A. Beethoven

B. Brahms

C. Fauré

D. Mendelssohn-Bartholdy

E. Rossini

F. Schubert

G. Wagner

H. Verdi

COMPOSITIONS

1. _____ "Aida"
2. _____ "The Barber of Seville" and "Stabat Mater"
3. _____ "Cantique de Jean Racine"
4. _____ "Christ on the Mount of Olives"
5. _____ "Elijah"
6. _____ "Fidelio"
7. _____ "The Flying Dutchman"
8. _____ "German Requiem"
9. _____ "Liebeslieder Waltzes"
10. _____ "Manzoni Requiem"
11. _____ "Miriam's Song of Triumph"
12. _____ "Missa Solemnis in D"
13. _____ "Nanie"
14. _____ "St. Paul"
15. _____ "Symphony No. 9" with a choral last movement

UNIT EXAM - Page 3
Romantic Era

Fill in the blanks

1. In 1815, _____ wrote two symphonies, two masses, four stage works, 140 songs, one string quartet, two piano sonatas, chorales, and extensive church music.

2. _____ moved from France to Italy to study with Palestrina and later wrote the opera, "Faust."

3. _____ was the great opera composer who wrote "Der Ring des Nibelungen" and had King Ludwig II of Bavaria as his patron.

4. From 1824 to 1895, _____ became director of the National Conservatory of Music in New York City.

5. _____ was born the same year as Wagner and composed the "Manzoni Requiem."

6. _____ composed the choral work "Cantique de Jean Racine" and died in Paris, France on November 4, 1924.

7. _____ became a cathedral organist in Linz, Austria, and later a professor in Vienna, Austria.

8. _____-_____ was the youngest of the famous "Russian Five," was a navy officer, and ultimately became Inspector of Music Bands of the Russian Navy Department.

Romantic Era

Match that Composer to His Country or Region of Origin

From the list of compositions below place the corresponding letter next to the name of its composer. Each country of origin may be used for one or more compositions.

COUNTRIES OR REGIONS OF ORIGIN

A. Austria
B. Belgium
C. Bohemia
D. France

E. Germany
F. Italy
G. Russia

COMPOSERS

1. _____ Balakirev, Mili

2. _____ Beethoven, Ludwig van

3. _____ Bellini, Vincenzo

4. _____ Bizet, Georges

5. _____ Borodin, Alexander

6. _____ Brahms, Johannes

7. _____ Bruckner, Anton

8. _____ Cui, César

9. _____ Donizetti, Gaetano

10. _____ Dvořák, Antonio

11. _____ Fauré, Gabriel

12. _____ Franck, César

13. _____ Gounod, Charles

14. _____ Mendelssohn-Bartholdy, Felix

15. _____ Mussorgsky, Modest

16. _____ Rimsky-Korsakov, Nicolai

17. _____ Rossini, Gioachino

18. _____ Schubert, Franz

19. _____ Schumann, Robert

20. _____ Smetana, Bedřich

21. _____ Verdi, Giuseppe

22. _____ Wagner, Richard

Dedicated to Jason Elam
and the Kearney, Missouri High School Choir

WENN SO LIND DEIN AUGE MIR
(*Liebeslieder-Walzer, Op. 52, No. 8*)
for SAB voices, with 4-hand piano accompaniment

Words by
Georg Friedrich Daumer (1800-1875)
Tr. Rick Weymuth

Music by
Johannes Brahms, 1870
Arranged by
RICK WEYMUTH

und so lieb - lich schau - et, je - de
and so fond - ly_____ gaze on me, ev - 'ry

und so lieb lich_____ schau - et, je - de
and so fond - ly_____ gaze_____ on me, ev - 'ry

und so lieb - lich schau - et, je - de
and so fond - ly gaze on me, ev - 'ry

grau - et.
trou - bled me.
Die - ser
This so

grau - et.
trou - bled me.
Die - ser Lie - be
This so beau - ti -

grau - et.
trou - bled me.
Die - ser Lie - be
This so beau - ti -

stie - ben!
die!

Nim - mer wird, wie ich, so treu
Nev - er will an - oth - er love you

stie - ben!
die!

Nim - mer wird, wie ich, so treu
Nev - er will an - oth - er love you

ben!

Nim - mer wird, wie ich, so treu
Nev - er will an - oth - er love

PRONUNCIATION GUIDE

Wenn so lind dein Auge mir und so lieblich schauet,
Wenn zoh leent dine ow-guh meer oont zoh leeb-lich shou-eht,

Jede letze Trübe flieht, welche mich umgrauet.
Yeh-duh leht-zuh Treu-buh fleet, vehl-chuh meech oom-grou-eht.

Dieser Liebe schöne Glut, laß sie nicht verstieben!
Dee-zehr Lee-buh scheu-nuh Gloot, lass zee neecht fehr-shtee-ben!

Nimmer wird, wie ich, so treu dich ein andrer lieben.
Neem-mehr veert, vee eech, zoh troy deech ine ahn-drehr lee-ben.

KEY
RENAISSANCE ERA

Answers to Renaissance Study Quiz #1

1) 1450, 1600   2) church   3) courts   4) harpsichord
5) medieval   6) voices, instruments   7) boys
8) males   9) vibrato   10) a cappella

Answers to Renaissance Study Quiz #2

1) F   2) A   3) E   4) D   5) B   6) G   7) C

Answers to Renaissance Study Quiz #3

S																			
T		L		P	R	I	N	T	I	N	G	P	R	E	S	S			
P		U																	H
E		T																	A
T		E				V	A	T	I	C	A	N							R
E																			P
R	C	H	R	I	S	T	O	P	H	E	R	C	O	L	U	M	B	U	S
S	S									E									I
B	I			D						N		F	L	U	T	E	S		C
A	S			R						A									H
S	T			U						I						M			O
I	I			M						S						E			R
L	N			S						S						D			D
I	E									A						I			
C	C	M	A	D	R	I	G	A	L	N						E			
A	H									C						V			
	A									E						A			
	P															L			
	E	N	A	T	I	V	E	A	M	E	R	I	C	A	N	S			
	L			R	E	C	O	R	D	E	R								

Answers to Renaissance Study Quiz #4

1) CLAVECIN   2) RECORDER
3) FINGER CYMBALS   4) HARPSICHORD
5) CHURCH ORGAN   6) CLAVICEMBALO
7) SPINET   8) VIRGINAL   9) VIOL
10) TAMBOURINE
11) PORTATIVE ORGAN   12) HAND DRUM
13) KRUMMHORN   14) LUTE   15) CLAVICHORD

Answers to Renaissance Study Quiz #5

1) printing press   2) one   3) di Lasso   4) des Prez
5) di Lasso   6) Dowland   7) Palestrina
8) Certon   9) Morley

Answers to Renaissance Study Quiz #6

P								N	O	T	R	E	D	A	M	E				T
A																				H
L		Q	U	E	E	N	E	L	I	Z	A	B	E	T	H					O
E																			W	M
S				M	I	C	H	E	L	A	N	G	E	L	O				I	A
T																			L	S
R		P		S	H	A	K	E	S	P	E	A	R	E					L	M
I	V	E	J																I	O
N	I	T	O		K	I	N	G	L	O	U	I	S						A	R
A	C	R	S																M	L
	T	U	Q															P	B	E
	O	C	U															O	Y	Y
	R	C	I															P	R	
	I	I	N															E	D	
	A															J				
		J	O	H	N	D	O	W	L	A	N	D				U				
																L				
P	I	E	R	R	E	C	E	R	T	O	N					I				
																U				
	O	R	L	A	N	D	O	D	I	L	A	S	S	O	S					

Answers to Renaissance Unit Exam

1) 1450, 1600   2) medieval   3) voices, instruments
4) harpsichord   5) boys, male sopranos
6) church   7) courts   8) males   9) di Lasso   10) vibrato
11) a cappella   12) printing press
13) unison or one part
14) des Prez   15) di Lasso
16) Dowland   17) Palestrina   18) Certon
19) Morley   20) de Victoria

KEY
Baroque Era

Answers to Baroque Study Quiz #1

	P	A	C	H	E	L	B	E	L			
										C		
			B	U	X	T	E	H	U	D	E	
			A						A			
V		P	U	R	C	E	L	L		R		
I		R		C				H		P		
V	A	M	O	N	T	E	V	E	R	D	I	
R	A	M	E	A	U				N			
L		T				H			T			
D		O			G	A	B	R	I	E	L	I
I		R			N				E		U	
F		I			D				R		L	
S	C	H	U	T	Z				E		L	
	S	S	C	A	R	L	A	T	T	I	Y	

Answers to Baroque Study Quiz #2
1) T   2) F   3) T   4) T   5) T   6) F   7) T

Answers to Baroque Study Quiz #3

	T						S			F		
R	A	V	E	N	S	C	R	O	F	T		R
	N						E					A
	N			M	O	R	A	V	I	A	N	N
	E		J				E					K
	N		A				N					L
	B		M				S					I
W	E	S	L	E	Y		O					N
	R		S				N					
	G		T			W	A	L	T	E	R	
	A		O									
	L		W									
P	E	N	N									
	M				P	U	R	I	T	A	N	S

Answers to Baroque Study Quiz #4
1) Scarlatti   2) Bach   3) Gabrieli   4) Purcell   5) Vivaldi
6) Charpentier   7) Lully   8) Praetorius   9) Buxtehude
10) Rameau   11) Handel   12) Monteverdi
13) Schütz   14) Pachelbel

Answers to Baroque Study Quiz #5
1) The Baroque era began.
2) The pilgrims arrived near Cape Cod on the ship,
   the *Mayflower*.
3) The Jamestown Colony was founded.
4) Henry Purcell wrote his opera "Dido and Aeneas."
5) Monteverdi wrote "Orfeo."
6) Marc-Antoine Charpentier was born near
   Paris, France.
7) Henry Purcell was born in Westminster, England.
8) The first pianoforte was built.
9) Handel wrote the "St. John Passion."

Answers to Baroque Study Quiz #6
1) 1607   2) "Bay Psalm Book"   3) William Penn
4) "The Grounds and Rules of Musick Explained"
or "An Introduction to the Art of Singing by Note"
5) "Introduction to the Singing of Psalm-Tunes"
6) John Wesley   7) Moravian   8) Bach's

Answers to Baroque Study Quiz #7
1) Handel   2) 20   3) father (and later brother)
4) opera   5) Arnstadt, Muhlhausen, Weimar   6) Cothen
7) Leipzig   8) Bach, Handel   9) 1750

Answers to Baroque Study Quiz #8
1) Bach   2) Zachow or Friedrich Wilhelm Zachow
3) 1726   4) oratorio   5) King George I of England
6) Choose three: "Acis and Galatea"; "Esther";
"Alexander's Feaste"; "Saul"; "Israel in Egypt"; "Messiah";
"Semele"; "Judas Maccabaeus"; "Jephtha"
7) "The Triumph of Time and Triumph"   8) Westminster

Answers to Baroque Study Quiz #9
1) G   2) H   3) E   4) I   5) B   6) J   7) A
8) D   9) F   10) K   11) C

Continued on Next Page

KEY
𝕭𝖆𝖗𝖔𝖖𝖚𝖊 𝕰𝖗𝖆

Answers to Baroque Unit Exam

Fill in the Blank: 1) 1607 2) "Bay Psalm Book"
3) "Introduction to the Singing of Psalm-Tunes"
4) John Wesley 5) Purcell 6) Vivaldi 7) Gabrieli
8) Schütz 9) Handel 10) harpsichord

Match the Composition to the Composer: 1) A 2) D
3) A 4) G 5) J 6) C 7) D 8) H 9) A 10) B
11) D 12) F 13) E 14) I 15) C

Match the Composer to the Country of His Origin:
1) E 2) E 3) E 4) A 5)D 6) E 7)B 8) D 9) C
10) C 11) D 12) D 13) C 14) D

Bach and Handel - Fill in the Blank: 1) King George I of
England 2) J. S. Bach 3) 20 4) Zachow or Friedrich
Wilhelm Zachow 5) father and brother,
Johann Christoph 6) oratorio 7) opera
8) Westminster 9) Leipzig 10) Bach

KEY
Classical Era

Answers to Classical Study Quiz #1
1) H 2) M 3) M 4) H 5) M 6) M 7) M 8) M
9) H 10) H 11) M 12) H 13) H 14) H 15) M

Answers to Classical Study Quiz #2
1) VIOLA 2) ORGAN 3) HARPSICHORD
4) CELLO 5) PIANO
6) VIOLIN 7) CLAVICHORD 8) DOUBLE BASS
9) GLASS HARMONICA

Answers to Classical Study Quiz #3
1) balanced, symmetrical 2) piano 3) Haydn, Mozart
4) 1750, 1825 5) continuous tonality

Answers to Classical Study Quiz #4
1) William Billings 2) Benjamin Franklin
3) Plantation owners 4) Francis Hopkinson
5) Moravians 6) George Gottfried Mueller
7) Francis Hopkinson

Answers to Classical Study Quiz #5
1) Rohrau 2) wheelwright 3) St. Stephen's
4) Michael 5) zero or no 6) Prince Paul Esterházy
7) Prince Nicholas Esterházy 8) Eisenstadt
9) "The Creation;" "The Seasons"
10) Choice of: Papa Haydn, Father of the Symphony,
Father of the String Quartet

Answers to Classical Study Quiz #6
1) 1756, 35 2) Archbishop Schrattenbach
3) Maria Anna or Nannerl 4) 3,720 5) Order of the
Golden Spur 6) six 7) Choice of: "Don Giovanni,"
"Cosi fan tutte," "La Clemenza di Tito," "The Magic
Flute" 8) "The Requiem" or "Requiem"
("Mass in D-minor, K. 626")
9) Süssmayr 10) 1791

Answers to Classical Study Quiz #7
1) M 2) H 3) M 4) H 5) H 6) M 7) H 8) M
9) H 10) H 11) M 12) H

Answers to Classical Era Unit Exam
Mozart and Haydn: 1) H 2) H 3) M 4) M 5) H
Composition to the Composer: 1) M 2) H 3) H
4) M 5) H
Fill in the blank: 1) Haydn, Mozart 2) 1750-1825
3) Benjamin Franklin 4) Francis Hopkinson 5) Francis
Hopkinson 6) St. Stephens 7) Prince Paul Esterházy
8) Eisenstadt 9) "The Seasons;" "The Creation"
10) Maria Anna or Nannerl 11) Order of the
Golden Spur 12) six 13) "The Requiem" or "Requiem"
("Mass in D-minor, K. 626")

KEY
Romantic Era

Answers to Romantic Study Quiz #1

	B	O	R	O	D	I	N				G	
	A									R	L	
	L	R	U	S	S	I	A			I	I	
	A									M	N	
	K		M	U	S	S	O	R	G	S	K	Y
C	U	I								K	A	
	R					B					Y	
	B	E	E	T	H	O	V	E	N	O		K
	V	U					S				O	
		F					T				R	
		T					O				S	
		S					N				A	
	L	A	W								K	
						M	A	S	O	N		
S	P	I	L	L	V	I	L	L	E		V	

Answers to Romantic Study Quiz #2
1) T 2) F 3) T 4) F 5) T 6) T 7) T 8) F 9) T

Answers to Romantic Study Quiz #3

B	R	U	C	K	N	E	R	S			V	
R						C					E	
A		F	R	A	N	C	K	H			R	
H								U			D	
M								M	B		I	
S	C	H	U	B	E	R	T	A	I			
				D	O	N	I	Z	E	T	T	I
	D			W		N		E				
	V			A		T						
G	O	U	N	O	D	G						
	R			N								
F	A	U	R	E		E						
	K			R	O	S	S	I	N	I		
M	E	N	D	E	L	S	S	O	H	N		
B	E	L	L	I	N	I		S	M	E	T	A	N	A

Answers to Romantic Study Quiz #4
1) SINGING SCHOOLS 2) TUFTS 3) LAW
4) BUCKWHEAT NOTES 5) DVOŘÁK
6) SAVANNAH 7) ST. LOUIS 8) MASON
9) SHAPE NOTES 10) MEDFIELD
11) SPILLVILLE

Answers to Romantic Study Quiz #5
1) The Romantic era begins.
2) Queen Victoria was crowned in England.
3) Felix Mendelssohn-Bartholdy wrote "Elijah."
4) Franz Schubert died on November 19.
5) First transcontinental railroad opened.
6) Verdi wrote the opera "Aida."
7) James Fenimore Cooper wrote the book "Last of the Mohicans."
8) Giuseppe Verdi wrote the opera "La Traviata."
9) The Civil War ends in the United States.
10) Music was added to the curriculum of Boston Public Schools.

Answers to Romantic Study Quiz #6
1) "Introduction to the Singing of Psalm-Tunes"
2) singing schools 3) schools, churches
4) Academy of Music 5) 1838 6) St. Louis
7) Andrew Law 8) Spillville

Answers to Romantic Study Quiz #7
1) Bonn 2) six 3) 1783 4) Count Waldstein 5) 1800
6) Symphony No. 9 7) "Fidelio"
8) "Christ on the Mount of Olives" 9) 1827

Answers to Romantic Study Quiz #8
1) Mendelssohn 2) Verdi 3) Fauré 4) Brahms
5) Dvořák 6) Gounod 7) Wagner 8) Schubert
9) Rossini 10) Brahms

Continued on Next Page

KEY
Romantic Era

Answers to Romantic Study Quiz #9

1) H   2) G   3) B   4) F   5) K   6) J   7) I   8) B
9) G   10) C   11) E   12) F   13) D   14) K
15) D   16) B   17) A

Answers to Romantic Study Quiz #10

1) VERDI   2) DONIZETTI   3) FAURÉ
4) MENDELSSOHN   5) DVOŘÁK
6) SCHUMANN   7) FRANCK   8) SMETANA
9) BIZET   10) SCHUBERT   11) BRAHMS
12) WAGNER   13) BELLINI
14) BRÜCKNER   15) GOUNOD   16) ROSSINI

Answers to Romantic Era Unit Exam

Beethoven, Brahms, and Mendelssohn: 1) metronome
2) six   3) "Symphony No. 9"   4) Count Waldstein
5) "Fidelio"   6) Mendelssohn, Brahms   7) Mendelssohn
8) Brahms   9) Brahms   10) Mendelssohn
Fill in the blank: 1) Schubert   2) Gounod   3) Wagner
4) Dvořák   5) Verdi   6) Verdi   7) Brückner   9) Rimsky-Korsakov
Match That Composition to the Composer:
1) H   2) E   3) C   4) A   5) D   6) A   7) G   8) E
9) B   10) H   11) F   12) A   13) B   14) D   15) A
Match That Composer to His Country or Region of Origin: 1) G   2) E   3) F   4) F   5) G   6) E   7) A   8) G
9) F   10) C   11) D   12) B   13) D   14) E   15) G   16) G   17) F   18) A   19) E   20) C   21) F   22) E